Conversations with Gwendolyn Brooks

Literary Conversations Series

Peggy Whitman Prenshaw
General Editor

Photo credit: © 2003 Nancy Crampton

Conversations
with Gwendolyn Brooks

Edited by
Gloria Wade Gayles

University Press of Mississippi
Jackson

www.upress.state.ms.us

The University Press of Mississippi is a member of the
Association of American University Presses.

Copyright © 2003 by University Press of Mississippi
Manufactured in the United States of America

11   10   09   08   07   06   05   04   03   4   3   2   1
∞

Library of Congress Cataloging-in-Publication Data

Brooks, Gwendolyn, 1917–
    Conversations with Gwendolyn Brooks / edited by Gloria Wade Gayles.
      p.   cm. — (Literary conversations series)
    Includes bibliographical references and index.
    ISBN 1-57806-574-7 (alk. paper) — ISBN 1-57806-575-5 (pbk. : alk. paper)
    1. Brooks, Gwendolyn, 1917– —Interviews.   2. Poets, American—20th
century—Interviews.   3. African American poets—Interviews.   I. Gayles,
Gloria Jean Wade.   II. Title.   III. Series.

    PS3503.R7244Z5235   2003
    811'.54—dc21
    [B]   2003047937

British Library Cataloging-in-Publication Data available

Books by Gwendolyn Brooks

A Street in Bronzeville. New York: Harper & Brothers, 1945.

Annie Allen. New York: Harper & Brothers, 1949.

Maud Martha. New York: Harper & Brothers, 1953.

Bronzeville Boys and Girls. New York: Harper & Brothers, 1956.

The Bean Eaters. New York: Harper & Brothers, 1960.

Selected Poems. New York: Harper & Row, 1963.

We Real Cool. Detroit: Broadside Press, 1966.

The Wall: For Edward Christmas. Detroit: Broadside Press, 1967.

In the Mecca. New York: Harper & Row, 1968.

Riot. Detroit: Broadside Press, 1969.

Family Pictures. Detroit: Broadside Press, 1970.

The World of Gwendolyn Brooks. New York: Harper & Row, 1971.

Aloneness. Detroit: Broadside Press, 1971.

Report from Part One. Detroit: Broadside Press, 1972.

The Tiger Who Wore White Gloves, or What You Are You Are. Chicago: Third World Press, 1972.

Beckonings. Detroit: Broadside Press, 1975.

A Capsule Course in Black Poetry Writing. With Keorapetse Kgositsile, Haki R. Madhubuti, and Dudley Randall. Detroit: Broadside Press, 1975.

Primer for Blacks. Chicago: Black Position Press, 1980.

Young Poet's Primer. Chicago: Brooks Press, 1980.

To Disembark. Chicago: Third World Press, 1981.

Mayor Harold Washington; and, Chicago, the I Will City. Chicago: Brooks Press, 1983.

The Near-Johannesburg Boy, and Other Poems. Chicago: David Company, 1986.

Blacks. Chicago, David Company, 1987.

Gottschalk and the Grande Tarentelle. Chicago: David Company, 1988.

Winnie. Chicago: David Company, 1988.

Children Coming Home. Chicago, David Company, 1991.

Contents

Introduction

We expect a search for interviews with Gwendolyn Brooks—both formal and casual, published and recorded—to yield a harvest commensurate with here stature as the first African American to win the Pulitzer Prize for poetry and one of the nation's most prolific poets. However, the number is surprisingly small, due primarily to Brooks's discomfort, by her own admission, in settings that require her to speak rather than to write. "I am a writer," she tells Paul Angle, "perhaps *because* I am not a talker." Studs Terkel found her to be both. Noting her concern, "in the beginning," that she might be inarticulate, he tells her, with almost palpable delight, "Oh, Gwendolyn Brooks, what things you were telling us about yourself! . . . [You] are truly articulate in what you write and even in the things you say with such economy." *Conversations with Gwendolyn Brooks* supports Terkel's sentiments, giving evidence that Brooks's talents in the interview merit attention, study, and praise.

Conducted between 1961 and 1994, the interviews in this collection took place in various settings—in radio recording studios and in university classrooms, in the coveted spotlight of an NEH celebration and in the intimacy of her living room—and yet Brooks seems unaffected by either place or audience. She is never ambiguous in her response to questions, and she makes no attempt to shield the private self from full view. Marriage, motherhood, divorce, financial difficulties, grief—she shares particulars of her life with candor, sometimes with humor, and never with sarcasm. She is a rapt, intense, and careful listener who sometimes directs the interviewer to questions never asked or rephrases questions with nuances she wants to examine. Her awareness of others, so emblematic of her art and her life, prevents the interviews from being heavily academic conversations between two people sitting rigid and self-important on a stage raised and spotlighted. Many have the feel of intimate gatherings in small rooms frugally furnished and accented with muted, but not faded, earth tones. In interviews that took place in university classrooms or at writers' conferences, Gwendolyn Brooks embraces the audience with the generosity of her spirit and with a genuine invitation for audience participation in the discussion. Attention to details, a singularly impressive contribution to the interviews, gives the impression that she is writing rough drafts of poems she will later revise. For her, there are no throw-away words, no minor chords of interest, no experience that is not invested in some way with potential material for the making of a poem.

Her disclaimer to the contrary, Gwendolyn Brooks seems at home in these interviews and, at times, grateful for opportunities they afford her: to acknowledge gifts from parents and friends, to examine both her art and her life, to celebrate the power and beauty of words, and to share with us her vision and hope for humanity. A humble and gentle woman, she does not alter what could be considered a recurring theme of the collective interviews and which, upon her death in 2000 at the age of eighty-three, the epitaph many scholars believe she would have chosen for her life: "I am an ordinary human being who is impelled to write poetry."

Of course, there was nothing ordinary about Gwendolyn Brooks. With no formal training in the writing of poetry and a diploma from a junior college, she earned some of the most prestigious literary honors in our nation: the Pulitzer Prize, the NEH Jefferson Lectureship, Poetry Consultant to the Library of Congress, and Poet Laureate of the State of Illinois, among others. She began writing at the age of seven, always knowing that she was a poet and never doubting that one day she would be published, a confidence she attributes primarily to supportive and encouraging parents—a mother who believed she would become a second Paul Laurence Dunbar and a father who filled their house with books and here memories with love. Brooks is clear, however, that she wrote, not because they encouraged her, but rather because, as she tells Roy Newquist, "I wanted to."

She was born in Topeka, Kansas, but she lived all of her life in Southside Chicago in the largest Negro area in the city—a world of kitchenette buildings. When Angle asks whether or not she will join other poets and move to New York, Brooks says, emphatically, that she will live in Chicago "in *my* forever," and for this reason: "It nourishes me." She was not always appreciative or, for that matter, aware of its significance to her creativity, having dreamed of living in the country and being nourished by nature lavishly present there, but conspicuously absent from urban life. In 1944, when an editor at Harper advised her "not to write disconnectedly about such things as love, death, and the mysteries of life, but to center my ideas in the background I really knew something about," she realized that a poet should be immersed in a milieu whose rhythms echo her heartbeat, whose images are reflected in the mirror of her reality. With this new awareness, and appreciation, she submitted a group of poems to Harper that became her first book of poetry, *A Street in Bronzeville.*

Interestingly, Brooks does not "try to evoke place" in her poetry. Rather, as she tells George Stavros, "I start with people." On the face of it, this comment seems to be contradictory, given her emphasis on the nourishment she receives from the world of kitchenette buildings, but the interviews, an excellent learning resource, give us a clarity about her art we would not otherwise have. They are replete with Brooks's analysis of some of her best loved works, among them *A Street in Bronzeville*, which has "humanity in it"; *Annie Allen*, the Pulitzer Prize volume, in which she was "impressed with the effectiveness of technique"; *The Bean Eaters*, her first "political" volume, some scholars maintain; *Maud Martha*, her only novel; *Report from Part One*, a slim autobiography; and *In the Mecca*, the volume she once considered her "blackest book yet." With the collected interviews serving as a "Sourcebook (or Casebook) on Gwendolyn Brooks," we understand that it is not the world of kitchenette buildings that inspires her, but rather women and men who meet the challenge of this world, some with despair and others with a humanity scholars have called heroic. Her intent as a writer, she tells Terkel, is "to put them down on paper." That intent produced portraits of black women and black men—ordinary and yet memorable—that constitute one of the most unique and remarkable galleries in American literature.

With quiet dignity, Brooks stands before portraits in selected poems, often challenging interpretations that have made their way into scholarship where they have remained somewhat unchallenged. For example, she challenges the interpretation of "The Mother" as "an abortion poem," pointing out a litany, so to speak of characteristics of motherhood that give the poem its richness and rhythms, and she explains that "The Life of Lincoln West" is not a poem about an ugly boy, but rather about a boy who rises above the notion of his "ugliness" to discover his beauty. She does not give currency to interpretations because they come from the mind, the pen, of scholars in the academy. For her, poetry belongs to the people, not to the critic, and to the reader, not to the poet, and the reader, she maintains, does not need to know critical theory in order to understand what the poet has created. A poem like "A Song in the Front Yard," she tells Susan Elizabeth Howe and Jay Fox, "just says what it wants to say and is not at all difficult to understand. You don't need to come upon it sneakily." Even poems imbued with subtleties of language, rightfully associated with her genius, are no less accessible to non-academic readers because readers bring "something to a poem," she tells Rebekah Presson.

They are "unique, different" individuals who make a poem "richer for [their] own use." To the poet belongs the creation of the poem. To the reader belongs the discovery of something the poet placed in the poem for him/her. In a real sense, the poet and the reader work together to give the poem its meaning. Such thinking is appropriate for a poet who does not believe in art for art's sake, a poem for poetry's sake, an elitist idea, in her opinion, that robs a poem of its true value by applauding difficulty and obtuseness and by locating a poem's value only in a time distant from the moment of now. She wants her poems to have meaning for this now-time and for all readers.

She sees every moment as pregnant with creative gifts, the interview no exception, and, therefore, Brooks is always writing. Even when she has neither time nor tools to do so, she is writing. Writing does not begin with inspiration from a Muse. She prefers not to believe in any such thing. It does not begin with a message. She is not a prophet. Nor does it begin with a model. She does not think "about . . . what anybody else in the world has done," she tells Stavros. Rather, for her, writing "begins with an idea or an impression." She becomes "excited about something" and "can hardly wait until she can get to the paper." And when she sits down to create the poem that is a word here or several lines there on little scraps of paper, she writes "as urgently" and "directly" as she can. Simply put, she tells Sheldon Hackney, she writes down "whatever comes—that's the beginning."

But it is only the beginning. Gwendolyn Brooks believes in revision, "a lot of revision," a necessary thing for a poet who weighs the possibility of every word. Writing is hard work or, in her words, "delicious agony" characterized by an ache for the right word and a reverent search for the right technique. She cannot predict—for what poet can?—how long it will take her to write a poem—fifteen minutes for some, fifteen months for others. She can predict, however, that when finally she releases the poem, she might feel compelled to return to it, bending "intently," again, "over the little phrase."

Hard work alone, however, does not make a poem effective. In fact, Gwendolyn Brooks believes the most worked-on, agonized-over, and revised poem can fail, and the poet should admit as much. Throughout the interviews, she calls her failures by title and by flaws. When a poem works—for example, "We Real Cool," her most popular poem, and "Gottschalk and the Grande Tarantelle," the title poem in her least known volume, that she considers successful—Brooks expresses pleasure and pride in what she has accomplished with words, rhythms, picture-painting, and technique, though always with humility. When a poem fails—as did so many in *Beckonings*, she says to Gloria T. Hull and Posey Gallagher—she explains why, without apology. It is in the nature of the creative process that language and technique sometimes miss the poet's mark, she believes, and, as well, that poets experience periods when "you are writing well as you see it and sometimes you're not." She is not convinced that poetry workshops are necessary for writing success or, for that matter, for the making of a poet. To be sure, they are useful in that they can teach a writer needed fundamentals about rhyme, meter form, and the like, helping the writer avoid clichés, mixed metaphors, over-alliteration (her weakness, she says), "free verse imperilings," and other traducers of effective poetry. But poetry workshops do not a poem make or a poet inspire. The same is true of education. A poet should get as much education as possible, but what the poet needs to do is read and read-read as much as he or she can and write as frequently as possible. In several essays, she repeats her belief that a poet can learn all he or she needs to know by reading. What a poet needs most of all is "to live richly with eyes open, and heart, too." A poem, she implies, comes from the heart, the soul.

While it is true the study of a writer's work over a period of years can reveal changes, if any, in style and philosophy, hearing a writer talk about her art in interviews conducted over a period of years makes such a revelation sharper and uncontestable. That is the case with the interviews in this volume. They not only reveal changes in Brooks's art and philosophy; they also name and date the experience that set the changes in motion. Brooks herself reports that she was transformed from a poet who happened to be Negro to a black poet, an African who writes poetry about black people and for black people whom, in the Ida Lewis interview, she identifies as "my people." The transformation began in 1967 at a Black Writers' Conference held at Fisk University, where, for the first time in her life, Gwendolyn Brooks, a dark-skinned black woman who had known the pain of rejection based on skin color, was in the midst of black poets who claimed the beauty of blackness. For the first time, she heard a new poetry forged into existence by the Civil Rights Movement. She experienced an epiphany; she was transformed.

The dates of the interviews serve as road signs in her journey to a more heightened racial consciousness. In the Terkel interview, conducted in 1961, Brooks makes no reference, even oblique ones, to race. She describes "the bean eaters" as "the great mass of eaters of beans"; the young men in "We Real Cool" as pool players at the Golden Shovel; and, in the 1961 interview with Angle, she says that "the preacher who ruminates behind the sermon" could be "any preacher." At the time, she was writing ballads and sonnets

and intoning the names of Dylan Thomas, T. S. Eliot and Yevgeny Yevtushenko, whom she considers a "good forerunner of what we may expect from
the future," she tells Newquist in that same year. At the time, she was teacher,
mother, wife, and not yet the heralded "mother" and mentor—indeed
queen— of *Sons of the Revolution*, young writers of the Black Arts Movement, most influential among them Don L. Lee (later Haki Madhubuti),
whose name rhythms like a chant in interviews that took place after 1967.

It is in the interview with Stavros, conducted in 1969, two years after the
Fisk Conference, that we see the first signs of her transformation. There is
controlled anger in the interview not present in the Terkel, Angle, and Newquist interviews, most noticeable when Brooks offers no apologies for writing about the world of kitchenette buildings. Noting that Faulkner was all
right writing about Yoknapatawpha, she suggests there are double standards,
racially influenced, in the question about her focus on Bronzeville. It is also
in the Stavros interview that we hear a new roll call of poets she considers
important. T. S. Eliot, Dylan Thomas, Marianne Moore, Robert Frost, and
e. e. cummings, among other European poets, have been replaced by Carolyn
Rodgers, Ron Milner, Walter Bradford, Etheridge Knight, Mari Evans, Nikki
Giovanni, Margaret Danner, Leroi Jones (later Amiri Baraka) and, most special of all, Don L. Lee (Haki Madhubuti). They baptized her whole in deep
waters of black consciousness from which she emerged bearing witness for
the empowerment, joy, and peace that comes from knowing self, loving self,
and being loved by her people.

Her world changed, and, to some extent, her aesthetics as well. Prior to the
Black Arts Movement of the sixties, she considered the polishing of technique to be "the most urgent duty of the Negro poet." She does not waver in
her belief that "a poet has a duty to words and that words can do wonderful
things," but she believes the new poets are liberating themselves from con-
straints on their creativity by "establishment" definitions of "good poetry."
What they are doing with language, form, and techniques, she believes to be
"a very healthy thing." While she champions their poetry, she has no interest
herself in writing "political" poems—how she hates the word! To be sure,
she sees herself writing poems different from those of her "Negro" period—
poems that are shorter and less "intellectual"; poems in which she experi-
ments with free verse, for these are "not sonnet times"; poems that will be
accessible in length, language, and form to the masses of black people wherever they are—in kitchenette buildings, in pool halls, in taverns. It is her
intent "to write a special kind of Gwendolynian poem," featuring song, she

tells Steve Cape. Her new poetry "will be songlike and yet properly called poetry."[1]

In addition to "Gwendolynian" poetry, Brooks demonstrated her commitment to the Black Arts Movement by becoming what some scholars have called the most visible and hard working nationally celebrated poet in American literary history. She leaves the community of "established" writers and readers and takes her art to people in Bronzevilles all across the nation. She conducts poetry workshops, gives public readings, establishes literary awards, and works in myriad ways to help bring into existence a second generation of black poets and to strengthen black publishers. In 1969, *Riot*, a departure from earlier volumes, was published by Broadside, a black press located in Detroit. Subsequent works, major among them *Report from Part One*, saw the light of day from black presses: Broadside, Third World, the David Company, and her own Brooks Press. She was the first nationally celebrated poet in the history of American letters to travel this route. It is a testament to her commitment to the new poetry and, as well, a testament of the new poets' respect for her genius that in interviews conducted after 1967 she refers less to the Pulitzer as the high point of her life and more to her inclusion in the Wall of Respect and to the establishment of the Gwendolyn Brooks Center at Chicago State University, the brain child of her poet son, Haki Madhubuti.

By the mid-seventies or early eighties, empowerment for women replaced black liberation in national headlines, forging into existence a feminist aesthetic and creating a group of black women writers whose artistic visions were shaped more by sensitivity to gender than to race. Gwendolyn Brooks was neither visible nor vocal in this group, a criticism that makes the Hull and Gallagher interview one of the most difficult in the collection. There is no question that gender was of secondary concern in Brooks's articulation of her poetic intent, as evidenced by her call in earlier interviews for bonding between black women and black men, a necessary thing for *racial* progress, and the problematic line in "Steam Song" about a man being a woman's necessary thing—a line she later deeply regretted. The fact that she is more of a *race woman* than a gender poet notwithstanding, she argues in her defense that women are prominent in all of her poetry, even in poems that predate the Black Arts Movement of the sixties. Opening the pages of several volumes, she offers her proof: many of her most anthologized poems, if not her signature poems, are portraits of women.

She defends herself again in the Claudia Tate interview and, paradoxically,

the subject is race rather than gender. Without recanting her passionate support for the Black Arts Movement or her gratitude for the immeasurable
impact it had on her life and her poetry, she seems to suggest that, though
she was transformed, she has not changed. As poet, she has always been, and
always will be, the Gwendolyn Brooks we hear in the Terkel, Angle, and
Newquist interviews: a poet who tenderly cares for words and who finds joy
in the mastery and mystery of the technique. She is weary of talk about the
"black aesthetic," the mantra of the Black Arts Movement. She does not say
the Movement is "dead" but, clearly, she is responding to a climate in which
the Movement is not a quickened thing. She is just as displeased with black
writers who write sloppily, demonstrating no commitment to language and
technique, as she is with black writers who indulge in literary "hair straightening," writing what the white establishment will publish. And she is impatient with anyone, regardless of race, who attributes the blackness in her
poetry to the Black Arts Movement of the sixties. Although she was a
"Negro" poet prior to 1967, she asserts that she has always written about
black people—naturally, without a "conscious intention." In her exchange
with Tate, Brooks comes across as more agitated than in any other interview
in the collection, her interview with Stavros and with Hull and Gallagher
being exceptions. In fact, she is so agitated that she is moved to do some
"fighting for myself," she tells Tate. If readers cannot see blackness in all of
her poetry, it is only because they do not have the patience "to sit down and
find out that in 1945 I was saying what many of the young folks said in the
sixties." She was transformed, and yet she remains a master of language and
technique. This exchange supports the opinion of Hull and Gallagher, with
which Brooks agrees, that she is caught in a duality that she had not resolved,
and probably cannot. It is a duality George Kent writes about in his biography
of Gwendolyn Brooks: she is an intellectual poet who wishes to be otherwise
in order to reach the masses of her people.

   In the sound of her gentle, small voice—we *hear* her in these interviews—
and the warmth of her responses, we experience her compassion and her
caring concern. We are not surprised, therefore, to learn in the Howe/Fox
interview that her "essential religion" is kindness or, in the Hackney interview, that she is an optimist who sees "real love in the world." As we close
Conversations with Gwendolyn Brooks, we are certain of this truth: she is
grateful for the impact the Movement had on her life and on her poetry,
especially as she experienced it through her mother-son relationship with
Haki Madhubuti. We leave the collection knowing that, before, during, and

after the Movement, she is "impelled to write poetry" and that her definition of poetry remains unchanged. From the first interview in the collection to the last, she believes, as she tells Kevin Bezner, that "poetry is life distilled" and that a poet has a duty to words. In the self-interview published in *TriQuarterly*, she says that a "poet is one who distils experience—strains experience. A poet looks—sees. Poets oblige themselves to see. Poetry is siren, prose is survey." We leave the collection knowing that this extraordinary woman and genius-poet, who is *indeed* black, takes delights and pleasure in being a poet, "a necessary and compulsory thing." As we leave the interviews, we know we will take with us all they taught us about her life and her poetry, the better to celebrate both.

GWG

Note

1. Steve Cape, "An Interview with Gwendolyn Brooks," *Artful Dodge* 1.2 (1979), 22–35.

I am indebted to Sylvia Lewis Baldwin, Janet Martin, Wanda Polite, and Alicia Smash at Spelman College for providing me with invaluable research and to Carolyn Aguila of Brooks Permissions for giving me informed and inspired guidance over a period of months. There is no doubt in my mind that her affection and reverence for Gwendolyn Brooks and her patience with my many queries made this book happen. I am indebted to my friend Carolyn Denard at Georgia State University for directing me to the University Press of Mississippi and to my sister Faye Henning at Simeon Career Academy for serving as my cook and chauffeur during my week of research at the Chicago Historical Society. But I am indebted in a most special way to Nora Blakely Brooks for giving me permission to reprint her mother's remarkable words. The generous spirit all of them demonstrated was fitting for a volume of conversations with a genius poet whose essential religion was kindness. I thank them. I thank them all.

Chronology

1917 Born 7 June in Topeka, Kansas, to David Anderson Brooks and Keziah Corine Wims Brooks.

1936 Graduates from Wilson Junior College in Chicago.

1938 Marries Henry Blakely.

1940 Gives birth to first child, a son named Henry.

1943 Wins the Midwestern Writers' Conference Poetry Award.

1945 *Street in Bronzeville*

1949 *Annie Allen*

1950 Awarded the Pulitzer Prize for Poetry for *Annie Allen*.

1951 Gives birth to a daughter named Nora.

1953 *Maud Martha*

1956 *Bronzeville Boys and Girls*

1960 *The Bean Eaters*

1963 *Selected Poems*

1966 *We Real Cool* (reprinted from *The Bean Eaters*)

1967 *The Wall*

1968 *In the Mecca*; named Poet Laureate of the State of Illinois.

1969 *Riot*; separates from Henry Blakeley.

1970 *Family Pictures*

1971 *The World of Gwendolyn Brooks*; *Aloneness*; "Black Steel: Joe Frazier and Muhammad Ali" commissioned for Joe Frazier/Muhammad Ali fight and printed in the official program for that event.

1972 *Report from Part One*; *The Tiger Who Wore White Gloves, or What You Are You Are*

1973   Reconciles with Henry Blakely.

1975   *Beckonings*; *A Capsule Course in Black Poetry Writing* (with Keora-petse Kgositsile, Haki R. Madhubuti, and Dudley Randall)

1976   Appointed to the American Academy of Arts and Letters

1980   *Primer for Blacks*; *Young Poet's Primer*

1981   *To Disembark*

1983   *Mayor Harold Washington; and, Chicago, the I Will City*

1985   Named Poetry Consultant to the Library of Congress.

1986   *The Near-Johannesburg Boy and Other Poems*

1987   *Blacks*

1988   *Gottschalk and the Grande Tarantelle*; *Winnie*

1991   *Children Coming Home*

1994   Named National Endowment for the Humanities Jefferson Lecturer.

2000   Dies in Chicago, Illinois, on 4 December.

Conversations with Gwendolyn Brooks

A Conversation with Gwendolyn Brooks

Studs Terkel / 1961

Broadcast on WFMT Chicago 3 January 1961. Reprinted by permission of Studs Terkel.

Gwendolyn Brooks reading "The Kitchenette Building."

ST: "The Kitchenette Building" as seen, observed if you will, poetized, by our guest, Gwendolyn Brooks, Pulitzer Prize winner living in Chicago. When we think of your poetry—and I suppose it's been described by many critics in so many different ways—but the honesty of it I suppose is the first word that comes to mind, the honesty and the simplicity of it. What do you feel when your poems are analyzed and criticized? What's your feeling?

GB: Well, I read with great interest everything that's said. I myself have only tried to record life and interpret it as I have seen it.

ST: As you have seen it. The poem we heard is from—was that your first volume of poetry, *A Street in Bronzeville*?
GB: Yes, in 1945.

ST: That was in 1945. You won the Pulitzer Prize for *Annie Allen*.
GB: Yes.

ST: That was some five years later?
GB: Yes.

ST: We think of the title itself: *A Street in Bronzeville*. This would—what basically would you say? This is a poetic record of your observations of the community itself?

GB: Yes, a record of my observations and, in some part, of my experiences. Certain things in all the books have happened to me or to people that I have known and—I've colored and interpreted as best I could.

ST: What of you, the creative artist herself? We think of you as Chicago. Was it always Chicago?

GB: Yes. I've always lived in Chicago. I was born in Topeka, but I prefer to think of myself as a Chicagoan because I was taken to Topeka to be

3

born—if I may put it that way—and when I was a month old, well, my mother brought me back to Chicago and I have been here more or less ever since.

ST: When was it poetry? The idea of poetry? The writing and reading of it? When did it come into your self life?

GB: My parents always saw to it that we had books in the house, and my mother took me to the library when I was about four or five. I enjoyed reading poetry, and I tried to write it. I think I was about seven at the time that I tried to put rhymes together, and I've loved it ever since.

ST: In your childhood memories or later years, was there any one or any kind of poet who you feel had the most impact upon you?

GB: In childhood years, I can't say. When I was twelve or thirteen, I began to be interested in Shakespeare and poets such as Wordsworth and Tennyson and Shelley, the conventional loves of youth, I believe, and first loves, I should say, because I think we all still admire those poets.

ST: If we may, I'm sure there will be a lot more questions that come to my mind and that of the audience as we hear you read some more of your work. We're with *The Street in Bronzeville* and we wander along and on page nine there's "hunchback girl: she thinks of heaven."

Brooks reads "hunchback girl: she thinks of heaven"

ST: I suppose there can be no true poetry without compassion, without understanding that you possess to such a degree and again as we think of "hunchback girl," we think, I suppose of. . . . It's probing too much, isn't it, to think of your own observations of people you've seen?

GB: No, it's not probing too much.

ST: Well, I was thinking of the preacher coming up but which I would love to do, if I may.

GB: Yes, I would like to hear you read.

Terkel reads.

ST: What of the preacher that ruminates behind the sermon? This one?

GB: Well, when I was younger—in fact, even to this day—I wondered and wonder what ministers in the pulpits are really thinking as they often say things that are rather conventional, sometimes cut and dried, and I've often wondered if they had any private feelings behind their words and that's why I wrote that poem.

ST: Private worldly feelings, perhaps.

GB: Yes, private worldly feelings, perhaps spiritual ideas other than those that they are giving us.

Terkel reads "the preacher: ruminates behind the sermon"

ST: I suppose—with you as with any genuine poet, Gwendolyn—the matter of looking at people, into their souls, if you will, their thoughts as in that case. . . . I think of the poem on page three of *The Street in Bronzeville*: "The Mother." Anything you care to say about this. You don't have to if you don't want to. I know it's a poem that you feel strongly about.

GB: Yes. Once again I was trying to understand how people must feel—in this case a mother who never really became a mother. This poem was the only poem in the book that Richard Wright, who first looked at it, wanted to omit, and he felt that a proper poem could not be written about abortions, but I felt otherwise and I was glad that the publishers left it in.

ST: At the time he wanted it omitted, but I'm wondering if in later years he would have felt that way about it? It's conjecture of course.

GB: I'd rather think he might have changed later.

Brooks reads "The Mother."

ST: Somehow, in thinking of "The Mother," we think of the next poem, too. You may read on page twenty of *The Street in Bronzeville*: "The Murder." And we think, too, of newspapers. When we think of newspaper reports of the coldness, the harshness in so many cases, the inhumanity of reports that deal with lives of people, events, I'm sure that the poem has found its way into news reports. I don't know what your basis was for writing it, but I'm sure there were many reports.

GB: "The Murder" does have an interesting background.

ST: Let's hear about "The Murder."

GB: This is something that happened in my own childhood right next door to me and on the street in Bronzeville. And there was only one difference: the mother was not gossiping down the street. She was working and the little boy really did keep asking when his brother was coming back. So I'll read it.

Brooks reads "The Murder."

ST: And so it seems in putting to poetry that which you've seen and that which you've heard about isn't a question of calling upon your fantasy life but upon the actualities of your own.

GB: Yes. That's what it has been.

ST: What of "Matthew Cole," the one I will try to read now?

GB: Well, that is based on the life of a friend of mine . . . my husband's. Oh, I first heard of him about fifteen years or so ago. Oh, longer than that. . . . seventeen or eighteen years ago.

Terkel reads "Matthew Cole."

ST: It seems, Gwendolyn, the whole world then is found really in Bronzeville, whether it's "Matthew Cole" or "The Event" or "The Mother," or whether it's the girl I like whose song in the front yard. . . .

GB: Well, that girl was me. My mother was very careful of her children, and at a certain time we had to come into the front yard and stay there. We couldn't go wandering down the block anymore. We used to envy the children who were free enough to do this. So I wrote.

Brooks reads "a song in the front yard."

ST: Oh, Gwendolyn Brooks, what things you were telling us about yourself. And you were wondering at the beginning, you said, you think you are inarticulate when it comes to. . . . Sometimes I am what is known as glib, but you are truly articulate in what you write and even in the things you say with such economy. Even now, I was thinking of this poem—your admiration for the rebel, too, is there. It seems to be there. . . .

GB: Yes, I believe I do have such an admiration in part at any rate.

Brooks reads "The Rebel."

ST: So, we've been just hitting a few of the poems, touching a few of the poems from *A Street in Bronzeville*. Then it was in 1949 that you wrote *Annie Allen*.

GB: Yes, it was published in 1949.

ST: And this was the one that—it was the Pulitzer Prize winner for poetry in 1950. What would you say is the difference? Do you sense a difference in yourself, in your interest in the five years between *The Street in Bronzeville* and *Annie Allen*?

GB: Yes, I think so. By the time I began to write *Annie Allen*, I was very much impressed with the effectiveness of technique, and I wanted to write poetry that was honed to the last degree that it could be. And I wanted chiseled wines, everything just right, real poetry I wanted to write, and that's the mood I was in when I began writing *Annie Allen*. I no longer feel that this is the proper attitude to have when you sit down to write poetry, but that's how I felt then.

ST: You say you no longer feel it's the proper attitude to have when you write poetry? What do you feel now?

GB: Well, I feel that my poems at any rate should be written more in the mood that I had when I wrote *A Street in Bronzeville*. I was just interested in putting people down on paper and although it is rougher than *Annie Allen*, I feel that there's more humanity in it.

ST: We'll come to your most recent work later and perhaps your feelings about that, *The Bean Eaters*, after we hear from *Annie Allen*. That won the big prize. There are sonnets here from part three of *Annie Allen*, the womanhood divided. Is there a reason for the division into sections here?

GB: Yes, I was trying to trace the life of a young woman, and I thought it was convenient to divide her . . . the first part of her life. I think she must have been about twenty-eight when the book ends.

ST: Before you read two of the verses from "Children of the Poor" . . . you met some of the poets who affected your very young girlhood.

GB: When I was about nineteen or twenty, I became interested in the moderns and I admired and still do admire Eliot and John Crowe Ransom, and a poet that isn't spoken of very much, but I think is a wonderful poet . . . Merrill Moore. He was a great sonneteer. I think he died only a few years ago. Have you heard that? He wrote thousands of sonnets.

ST: You mentioned sonnets. Here then, the sonnet, "Children of the Poor."

Brooks reads "Children of the Poor."

ST: "The Rites for Cousin Vit." I know you chose this. You like this very much. In reading it, I, of course, am crazy about it. What about "The Rites for Cousin Vit"?

GB: Well, that, too, is based on a real happening. Vit—of course that wasn't her name—was a friend of mine who had that impressibility that seems unconfinable even in death and that's why I wrote

Brooks reads "Rites for Cousin Vit."

ST: Oh yes. Well, somehow of Cousin Vit, I thought of Bessie Smith. Do you mind hearing this music played as sort of a commentary on your poems?

GB: I was just thinking how effective the music is. It just seems inevitable.

ST: In this, the irrepressibility, the irrepressibleness of your Cousin Vit . . . you might say Vit conquers death really. Is that what you're saying there?

GB: In a way, yes.

ST: And so, we feel that about "Queen Bessie," too. There's old laughter opposite that, and this, I suppose, is a question of timelessness because, though you wrote this back in 1950. . . .

GB: I didn't write this poem in 1950. I wrote it when I was about nineteen.

ST: Oh, you did? I didn't realize that.

GB: And, of course, I don't know anything about Africa. I have never been there, have never been that fortunate but this is just a childhood impression that I had of Africa based on perhaps nothing.

ST: Harpers has always been your publisher. Haven't they?

GB: Yes.

ST: *The Bean Eaters* is available now.

GB: Yes. It was published in 1960. April.

ST: And this is just a tip to the listeners who want a poetry that is poetry truly. *Bean Eaters.* Before the book itself begins is a dedication here, Gwendolyn, "Dedication to David Anderson Brooks, my father." Anything you care to say about this dedication?

GB: Well, it doesn't have any reference to the book itself, but my father died just about the time that the book was about to be published, and I wanted naturally to honor him in some way and so I quickly sent this poem to the publisher.

ST: Was he an influence in some way?

GB: Oh, my father was a wonderful man and he was devoted to poetry and music. He read a great deal and told my brother and myself stories from earliest childhood and sang to us wonderful ballads and read wonderful old poems. Plus, he had a tremendous influence on our lives.

Brooks reads poem.

GB: Oh, how wonderful (reference to playing of "Deep River" sung by Roland Hayes).

ST: You said your father liked Roland Hayes.

GB: Yes, he did and he would have been so happy to have heard that attached to . . . well, it's impossible, isn't it?

ST: What of *The Bean Eaters*? Is this a return to that humanity you felt was in *A Street in Bronzeville*. Less of the fineness of *Annie Allen*. You said something about this earlier.

GB: Yes, in a way, I think that's true. To tell you the truth, I haven't quite decided how I feel about this book yet. I myself enjoy *A Street in Bronzeville* more than any of them, but several people have said *The Bean Eaters* shows an advance and interest in the quality of the human condition. I haven't quite decided yet.

ST: Why *The Bean Eaters*? What's the significance of the title?

GB: Well, I was referring to the great mass of eaters of beans, people who are not rich, who don't eat lobster as a rule but chiefly resort to beans.

ST: "We Real Cool" on page 17. There is a little note above the poem: "The Pool Players 7 at the Golden Shovel."

GB: Yes, it's about pool players.

ST: There they were.

Brooks reads "We Real Cool."

ST: Of course, I'm so taken with the rhythm of your reading. Would you mind telling us about that?

GB: Well, ideally, for myself at any rate, the "we" is supposed to be almost attached to the word that precedes it, and it's to indicate a sort of lost-ness and a sort of bewildered clutch at identity, a sort of—a little cry: *we*. And yet this "we" can't come and stand up straight and tall. It's not in. . . . These pool players feel that way, although I'm sure that most of them wouldn't be able to express it.

ST: What you have in this very brief poem . . . it has its rhythm, too. Rhythm of them, the very rhythm, and at the same time what you're offering is their lost-ness. Sixty-two. Now we come to another aspect of Gwendolyn

Brooks. It's part of a continuity, a very natural one. "The Ballad of Rudolph Reed." This is an actual event, isn't it? Would you mind. . . .

GB: No, it's not an actual event.

ST: Wasn't it?

GB: No, this is pure imagination—of course based on things that have happened or can happen.

ST: Oh, I thought there was a Rudolph Reed. This is pure imagination but based upon some events that were similar to it.

GB: Yes, for example—of course you can think of Trumbull Park although I don't believe there were any deaths out there, but there could have been. That's what I meant.

ST: Now you write this poem as almost a traditional child ballad, as a ballad, for the form itself is an old time ballad form.

GB: Yes.

ST: May I try reading this?

GB: Please.

Terkel reads "Rudolph Reed."

ST: I was thinking, Gwendolyn, as I was reading this . . .

GB: And you read it very well.

ST: Thank you. The power of this ballad—I think of . . . somehow the rhyme, the scheme . . . I think of "Rime of the Ancient Mariner" and "Sir Patrick Spence." Have you heard of it?

GB: I've heard of it. Yes.

ST: As you wrote, did you have—aside from the content and the passion of it—were you thinking of old English ballads?

GB: No, not by this time. I have admired the ballad form for so many years. Once I get started, get a line, like "Rudolph Reed was oaken"—well, the rest just follows automatically. I love the ballad form.

ST: "I am not hungry for berries, I am not hungry for bread, but hungry, hungry. . . ." Here is "Sir Patrick Spence," the old, old ballad. I think there's a form here that's similar to it, has that same power, like it's through the ages feeling . . . if we may just hear a piece of this.

Terkel plays recording of "Sir Patrick Spence."

ST: Since you say this is based upon what might have been, there is a poem you hesitate to read—"A Bronzeville Mother Loiters in Mississippi. Meanwhile, a Mississippi Mother Burns Bacon"—because you heard Ruby Dee, that beautiful actress, read it on. . . .

GB: Yes, a few months ago. She read it on a program, *Camera 3*, and she so beautifully translated my own thoughts that ever since I've rather hesitated about reading it myself.

Brooks reads the poem.

ST: I thought again that here, too, there's reference made to a ballad. If we can perhaps open this with the name of the poem: "A Bronzeville Mother Loiters in Mississippi. Meanwhile, a Mississippi Mother Burns Bacon."

GB: Well, the events in this poem are a little sturdier, I believe, than those in that beautiful ballad. They—it's the story, of course, of the murder of Emmett Till.

Brooks reads "The Last Quatrain of the Ballad of Emmett Till."

ST: Imagine, Gwendolyn Brooks, your poem about this woman and about this man and about the boy who isn't there and yet is there and about his mother who isn't there and yet is there says so much more than I imagine a tome or any kind of treatise on the subject. Isn't this the poet's job? The poet gets to say what he wants to say pretty much.

GB: Yes, to condense and to make concise, I believe. To refine.

ST: To refine and to intensify and these are but a few of the poems from *The Bean Eaters* that is so beautiful and so eloquent. It's Harper and Brothers, and it's available now and perhaps to end this hour with you, Gwendolyn Brooks, the title poem itself. You spoke of the bean eaters being not the fine prince or the fine princess but so many of the people.

Brooks reads "The Bean Eaters."

ST: They, too have their own nobility, a special kind. Gwendolyn Brooks, thank you very much for giving of your art, your reading, your poetry, your time.

GB: Thank you.

ST: The three books of Gwendolyn Brooks are *A Street in Bronzeville, Annie Allen* that won the Pulitzer Prize in 1950, and her new book that a number of critics consider her finest, though you still lean toward *A Street in Bronzeville*, you yourself do.

GB: At present.

ST: At present. Gwendolyn Brooks, thank you very much indeed for being our guest.

GB: Thank you.

An Interview with Gwendolyn Brooks

Paul Angle / 1967

From *Report from Part One* (Detroit: Broadside Press, 1968), 20–25.
Reprinted by permission of the Estate of Gwendolyn Brooks.

Angle: How did you happen to become a writer?

Brooks: I always enjoyed reading when I was a child. Pretty soon, I suppose, it occurred to me that it might be wonderful if *I* could create something, too. I began putting rhymes together when I was seven, so I'm told by my mother. And continued. I was encouraged by both my mother and my father.

Angle: At what stage in your life, if you can identify it, did it appear to you that you could become a professional writer?

Brooks: I have never liked the phrase "professional writer." I haven't thought of writing in that sense. Indeed, one who chooses to become a poet does well not to think of money or even of making a living by writing of verse. I wrote because I wanted to. I knew I'd always compose poetry, whether it was published or not.

Angle: I'm sure that the term "professional writer" isn't a very good one. And yet could we use it in the sense of one's work being published?

Brooks: I would not say so, because I feel that a writer should be very selective about what he publishes. And if he is selective he isn't going to have a great deal to publish. But I'm thinking primarily of poets. I can't conceive of a "professional" poet. Well—Edgar Guest, perhaps?

Angle: I suppose you're right. Nevertheless, I had a reason for asking my question. In the last two or three years of his life I knew Vachel Lindsay. I was living in Springfield at that time and he was most irate because the city directory people didn't want to list him simply as "poet," which he contended he was. Anyhow, I use the term "professional" for a steady writer whose works are published. Was it always your ambition from childhood to write, or was it a compelling necessity rather than an ambition?

Brooks: It was a necessity. *Ambition* doesn't seem a proper word to describe what I felt as I grew up and continued to write. I enjoyed it very much, and I was convinced that it would be good to "enchant" others with these products of MY MIND. Once, I considered *burying* my precious manuscripts in the back yard so that in the future—at some time in the hundreds of years to come—they would be discovered and loved.

Angle: You wrote because you wanted to.
Brooks: Yes.

Angle: And you still write because you want to?
Brooks: Yes, I still write because I want to, but there is a difference now. Recently, I confided to friends how much more fun writing was in those years of my youth, when I had no publishing prospects. I was free. If things were not "right," what difference did it make? But now, when I have pretty good prospects of having what I write published, I'm very concerned. I want to be sure that everything is good, and this imposes a constraint.

Angle: Do you find writing hard work?
Brooks: Yes. It is hard work. It gets harder all the time.

Angle: Partly because of the compulsion you have to come as close to perfection as you think you're capable of coming?
Brooks: That's true.

Angle: Now let me ask you another question. It is said that during much of his career Marcel Proust wrote in a windowless, sound-proof room, shutting himself off from not only intrusion, but also from humanity insofar as it was possible for him to do so. Could you write under such circumstances? Or would you want to write under such circumstances?
Brooks: Yes, I would enjoy it. That's one of my problems—finding extended privacy. I'm thinking now of going away at the end of summer—*some* summer—to a hotel in which I would have just such a situation. I would stay in my room, and have my meals delivered; and I would write, write, write.

Angle: That sounds pretty good. But in fact you do have to write in an environment. You cannot, month in and month out, exclude the surroundings in which you live.
Brooks: No. I cannot.

Angle: Now, do you find that environment—and let's use the term in a broad sense—encouraging, thwarting, or of no significance?
Brooks: You say do I find the environment encouraging, thwarting or. . . .

Angle: Of no significance—having no effect upon the creative process.

Brooks: You don't have noise in mind, do you?

Angle: No, something else.

Brooks: Then I have to say that I find I am not disturbed by my environment. In my twenties when I wrote a good deal of my better-known poetry I lived on 63rd Street—at 623 East 63rd Street—and there was a good deal of life in the raw all about me. You might feel that this would be disturbing, but it was not. It contributed to my writing progress. I wrote about what I saw and heard in the street. I lived in a small second-floor apartment at the corner, and I could look first on one side and then on the other. There was my material.

Angle: I think this experience comes out in some of your poems of this period. So the human environment in which you have lived has contributed to your poetry and has not affected it adversely.

Brooks: No, indeed, it hasn't affected it adversely, but has helped me.

Angle: How about personal contacts? I mean by that: do you feel it is desirable for you to be in frequent touch with other writers?

Brooks: No. When I was young I belonged to writing groups and I drew a lot from them. I tell young writers today that it is fine to belong to a writing group. You can derive sustenance from your fellows. That's all very helpful. But when you are older it is likely that you will want no more of such "togetherness."

Angle: Do you feel that the fact that you are a writer sets you apart from other people?

Brooks: No. No, I have never felt this. I am a human being who enjoys writing poetry.

Angle: And other people do not consider you to be rather peculiar?

Brooks: Oh, all along people have considered me to be "rather peculiar." When I was a teen my teen friends wondered, as they partied and danced, why I was happy to stay in my tiny room and write. They thought this was very odd and that I was doomed to failure, that I would never have boy friends, a marriage, children. Even now many who admire the things that have happened to me do not regard me with entire seriousness. "I must finish this," I tell them. "I must start that . . . I can't go here, I can't go there. . . ." "You can interrupt what you're doing," they seem to feel. "It's only pen and paper."

Do you believe, as I do, that it is not the *instinct* of man to love Art? Man will have occasional recourse to Art, may admire, may respect, may salute. May gasp. But in the presence of Art man is not continuously comfortable. Christmas is Art. A funeral is Art. But in almost every instance man is glad to get away, to spread his arms, to shake, dog-like, to shout "I'm *free*."

Angle: I know something of your feeling because I have had the experience myself, not in Chicago but in smaller towns. Because I was spending so much time writing people rather looked at me with some degree of—I would like to say wonderment—but I think *pity* would be the better word. I wondered whether this was your experience. Apparently it is not.

Brooks: I have said that many people do feel that there is something strange about being a writer and about being content to remain a writer. On the other hand I have said that I do not feel *apart* from other people. I am an ordinary human being who is impelled to write poetry.

Angle: I suppose what I'm trying to lead up to is this question: Is the Chicago environment conducive to a writing career? Or does it have any effect on you one way or the other?

Brooks: I've always lived in Chicago, so I have no good basis for comparison. When I was a child I used to think that I would write better if I lived in the country. I'd see movies where children were running in the country and picking flowers. I'd meet people who knew the names of flowers and the names of trees and the names of birds. That was fine. But I feel now that it was better for me to have grown up in Chicago because in my writing I am proud to feature people and their concerns—their troubles as well as their joys. The city is the place to observe man *en masse* and in his infinite variety.

Angle: And this city furnishes you an environment which you find entirely satisfactory as far as your own career is concerned. It does not impede you as a writer in any way?

Brooks: It nourishes.

Angle: So you would have no desire to follow the example of so many Chicago writers and head off to New York?

Brooks: No, I intend to live in Chicago for *my* forever.

Angle: Do you think that the fact that you are a Negro placed you under any handicap in a writing career?

Brooks: If it has, I don't know about it. Certain things might have happened that I don't know about, but I can't say that I have been hindered, because of my race, in the field of writing. I am not aware of this being true. I have written poems. I have submitted the poems to editors and publishers. When the poems were poor they were returned (as a rule!). When they were other than poor they were published. Everything that I have written that I wanted to see published has been published, with the exception of one juvenile which needs a couple of adjustments. And for many years I have had writing invitations from editors and publishers.

I have something further to say on the subject, however. I do believe that it is true, as Karl Shapiro says, that many white anthologists will not admit black writers to their pages. Mr. Shapiro wrote (in a foreword to Melvin Tolson's "Harlem Gallery"): "One of the rules of the poetic establishment is that Negroes are not admitted to the polite company of the anthology. Poetry as we know it remains the most lily-white of the arts."

There are exceptions to my exceptions, of course. Sometimes Paul Laurence Dunbar, Langston Hughes, Countee Cullen, and James Weldon Johnson may be found. Sometimes I may be found. Sometimes LeRoi Jones may be found. Rarely or never Kent Foreman, Don Lee, Dudley Randall, Margaret Danner, David Llorens, Ted Joans, G. C. Oden, Julia Fields, Robert Hayden, Conrad Rivers, Owen Dodson, Margaret Walker. (You will find these people in the *Negro* anthologies, in Hughes's and Bontemps's anthologies.)

Angle: What is your feeling about the Civil Rights movement?

Brooks: First of all I must say that I am not a social scientist. I like to refer the interested to Lerone Bennett, Hoyt Fuller, or John Henrik Clarke, whose minds I respect. I am impressed constantly by my acquaintances that the important thing is to have statistics, and I do not have statistics. I can merely say that I think it is necessary, this movement, and that it was bound to *evolve* sooner or later. Sooner or later there was bound to be an accelerated press for civil rights. I am surprised it did not happen before it did. The impatient seeds, of course, were always about. Has *any* oppressed and repressed group endured outrage, without a yip, *forever*?

Angle: Do you think there has been real progress in the last twelve or thirteen years towards civil rights? Toward equality of status, toward equality of opportunity?

Brooks: There has been progress, yes, with most of the advance initiated or stimulated (pleasantly or unpleasantly) by the black man himself. But the thing that is stressed by the people who have their hearts and bodies on the line is that progress, a little bit more each year, is not enough. The point is that people are people and they have "inalienable rights." (Where have I heard *that* before?) The civil rights situation is like a pregnancy. It will get worse, I believe, before it gets better. What the usual pregnancy comes to is a decent baby. That is what we all hope will be the end product of this stress. It is customary, at the end of a pregnancy, to have for your pains a decent baby.

Angle: A decent society in which no distinction is made between people of color. And that is the end or goal of the civil rights movement.

Brooks: Insofar as I know. But I must "announce" that there is an auxiliary problem. I must "announce" that many Negroes (they prefer to be called *blacks*, simply; for where, they ask, is "Negroland"?) no longer want any part of even *wonderful* whites. They have suffered so many crushes that now they are turning to themselves (finding "white" there too and feverishly scraping it out!) And they love blackness. They make a banner of blackness. What will be the end, as regards this intensifying compulsion? I am not able to tell you. When white and black meet today, *sometimes* there is a ready understanding that there has been an encounter between two human beings. But often there is only, or chiefly, an awareness that Two Colors are in the room.

Angle: Do you believe that the aforementioned goal is attainable within the reasonable future? You see I'm using some pretty broad terms that are not very clearly defined.

Brooks: I do feel that it is attainable, but I couldn't say when it will be achieved, because I don't know what the people of either race will be doing in the near future. I can't say that the agitation will end in ten years, or twenty years, or one hundred years.

Angle: Would you care to say anything more on this subject? I am talking to you primarily as a writer, but I think the civil rights movement has a relationship to a writing career. Not perhaps yours, but you are not likely to find, I would think, very many Negro writers, unless basic education improves. You would agree, I suppose, that a certain fundamental education of good quality is essential as far as writing is concerned?

Brooks: Yes, I believe that a writer, as well as anyone else, should have as much education as he can manage. I urge those children who ask me "How do you become a writer?" to stay in school, of course, and along with that, to read as much as possible. The book-involvement afforded by today's schoolhouse is *not* sufficient, because no curriculum is complete.

Angle: Is the poet affected by today's social unrest?

Brooks: The poet, first and foremost an individual with *a* personal vision, is also a member of society. What affects society affects a poet. So I, starting out, *usually* in the grip of a high and private suffusion, may find by the time I have arrived at a last line that there is quite some public clamor in my product.

Angle: Let's change the subject. We have been talking in terms of the Chicago environment. What do you think could be done in Chicago to further writing?

Brooks: Most of the colleges are becoming more and more interested in fostering creative writing, and many of them have writers-in-residence. I have creative writing classes, currently, in three colleges here: Elmhurst College, Columbia College, and Northeastern Illinois State College. There is a good deal of activity of that kind now in and about the city.

Angle: Do you think a person can be taught to write? In the light of your own experience?

Brooks: There are certain hard specifics that can be taught. Sonnet rules. Guards against free verse imperilings. Iambic pentameter. When I was twenty-three, I joined a poetry-writing group organized and led by Inez Cunningham Stark, of whom you may have heard. Dead now, she was a familiar art figure here for decades. At the time, she was a reader for the magazine *Poetry*. She came to the Southside Community Art Center and taught us many things about modern poetry. That was an aspect of her effort that helped me the most. At that time, I was subscribing too obediently to the older poets. She introduced me to many of the moderns.

Angle: Has this had a beneficial effect upon your writing?

Brooks: I believe so, yes. I learned to fear the cliché.

Angle: Let me ask you about *Poetry* magazine. Do you think it plays a significant role in the cultural life of Chicago?

Brooks: I hope *Poetry* magazine will always be here. (I especially like its habit of accepting manuscripts only from newcomers, in the summer months.) I do think that it would be fine to have other magazines, too. I think we are in great need of more literary magazines of high quality.

Angle: The universities are doing something along that line.

Brooks: *Tri-Quarterly* at Northwestern, edited by Charles Newman, is important.

Angle: I think you've answered the main, primary questions that I wanted to ask. Now let me summarize your statements, and see if you would like to amplify or correct them. You find Chicago a perfectly satisfactory place in which to work, as a writer—except for the immediate problems of privacy which all of us have to struggle with. Am I correct in that? You have no quarrel with it.

Brooks: I favor this environment for myself. The kind of work that I am doing needs a busy city as a background.

Angle: And you do not feel you, as a Negro, are under any disadvantages in writing.

Brooks: I would say that you put that question a little differently before. As I remember, you asked me if being a Negro has adversely affected my "career." That's what I was answering. My answer continues to be no. Indeed, listen to this—once a well-known poet, Ralph Pomeroy, told me he envied me very much, because *I* would "never have to go in search of a theme!" To pursue the subject: when I was thirteen, or twelve, I began sending manuscripts to magazines. Most of them came back, and they *should* have come back. Not until I was twenty-one or twenty-two did I write any poems that I would want seen today.

I can't say that the manuscripts came back because I was Negro; they came back because they were not good. That is my experience. Now, you might get different answers from other writers of my race, and properly so; but that is what I have to say about my own experience.

Angle: And you think that there are feasible ways to encourage and stimulate writers—ways that we are not exploiting to anything like their possibilities at the present time, both in Chicago and the state of Illinois.

Brooks: Yes. I do have this evil, poisoning side-observation to make: There are too many books already!

Angle: Would you mind putting your convictions in your own words?

Brooks: I feel that awards and fellowships are very encouraging to writers. They offer writers the most important asset of all—time in which to write. And I feel that these advantages might be fostered by the state or by such organizations as the Illinois Arts Council, the Mayor's Cultural Committee, and by the schools. I feel that a good deal of work can be done in the primary grades to encourage development of the talents that will be imposing in our immediate future.

Angle: That's interesting. I never thought of that possibility in the primary grades. I have assumed that the secondary schools, the high schools, were the places in which to do it.

Brooks: I get a more exciting response from the elementary schools. I've sponsored contests in two elementary schools and two high schools. Cornell and Burnside schools and Hirsch and Marshall high schools. The younger children were *basic*, the high school students were *careful*. I think it's good to get them while they are young and encourage. . . .

Angle: Self-expression?

Brooks: I want to use the word "freshness." It is good to foster the freshness that they have.

Angle: Well, maybe you'll think of a better word. It's pretty good as far as I'm concerned.

Brooks: I am a writer perhaps *because* I am not a talker! It has always been hard for me to say exactly what I mean in speech. But if I have written a clumsiness, I may erase it.

Angle: How important do you think the correct use of the English language is for a writer?

Brooks: I feel that it is absolutely commendable! Is there a special reason for asking me this?

Angle: Yes. So many people seem to think that they don't have to be very careful about the language, that on newspapers copy editors will clean it up and that in publishers' offices tenses will be made to agree. So they write in slovenly fashion.

Brooks: Is that right? I certainly don't approve of it. Language should be used with care and precision.

Angle: What about style? What about Ezra Pound? Many of his writings have no relationship to correct grammatical usages. Am I right?

Brooks: I thought that Ezra Pound was a master of English—that he knows what to do with words.

Angle: The grammar that he uses. . . .

Brooks: Where there are "veerings," I'm sure they are intended—done for a special reason. I can't think of a poem just now that he has written in which anything was amiss. Grammatically speaking!

Angle: Let's talk a little more about Chicago. We have here the mayor's Committee for Economic and Cultural Development. It has a subcommittee concerned primarily with the cultural life in Chicago. What do you think that group, either by itself or by stimulating other groups, could do to make writing more productive? Is it a matter of awards, fellowships, or what? I think you have pointed out somewhere that we are much more inclined to support and subsidize music and the performing arts than we are to subsidize the individual creativeness of the author.

Brooks: That is true. I think that beginnings must be made with the young. Let us *take* art to those who are not going to get it otherwise. I believe, for instance, creative writing workshops for the very many interested young would be rewarding. I am working in this way now through Oscar Brown's Alley Theatre projects on the South Side of Chicago, and the talent I find is exciting, the eagerness inspiring. I don't believe that such groups should be masterminded by their adult initiators indefinitely, and I'm assisting one of the young men in the group to take over my "duties" when a year has passed. I would like him to emphasize, especially, involving some of the very able members of South Side teen gangs.

Angle: I would like to apply my general question, if it is possible to do so, to creative writing. I remember attending a luncheon of a group which makes annual awards to writers. It had just given an author $1,000 in recognition of a newly published book. He remembered that the money would have done him five times as much good when he was writing the book as it did coming after publication. That's the trouble with awards.

Brooks: I think the schools might do something along this line. As I have said, I sponsored poetry competitions in South Side and West Side schools a few years ago, and the children seemed very eager to write and to express their thoughts. The schools that allowed the contests seemed willing to cooperate. Teachers did the judging; I refuse to do that. Reports were gratifying. I think more of this sort of thing might be done throughout the city.

Angle: Would you think that the schools are the best medium, perhaps, for teaching and encouraging writing?

Brooks: Not necessarily. I think that people such as myself, in the field of writing, could very well become involved personally, as well as financially, and encourage and assist these young people from whom our future talents may be expected.

Angle: And you think this could be done throughout the state?

Brooks: Yes, I do. There are small orchestras here and there, and there are painting societies, and I think that writing should not be neglected. There is much "art money" in Illinois. Very little of it is apportioned to writers. Very little of it is spent in ways that will encourage a favorable climate for effective literary activity. Money should go *straight* to the people who can use it creatively and forthwith.

Angle: The orchestras and the painting groups do seem to have readier entree to supporting funds than has the writer.

Brooks: I wonder why that is?

Angle: I suppose it could be a matter of mechanics. The orchestra is an established and tangible thing. The writer is struggling in his own study with a manuscript which perhaps nobody knows about. How are you going to reach him, and help him at the critical stage when he really needs help? When he is collecting rejection slips he doesn't know whether he can afford to go on or not. All too often he is working at a full time job and trying too write at nights and over weekends. How can you encourage him to persist in the strong uphill fight that writing all too often turns out to be?

Brooks: I believe we have to make it known that we are willing to help. We writers who are more or less "established"—hateful word—must declare our disposition to assist, must draw out the hidden struggler. Fellowships might be given by the state or the city; and large awards will bring out many talented writers whose existence has never been suspected!

Angle: Of course such awards are being given, and the most substantial ones are being offered today by quite a few publishers.

Brooks: Good.

Angle: Unfortunately, we do not have many Illinois publishers. We have some very good ones, but nothing like the number you will find in New York. Of course, these awards are not limited to geographical locations.

Brooks: I suggested to the Illinois Arts Council, of which I was a member, that it would be a fine thing to give a very large award here, which would be called "The Illinois Arts Award," or—

Angle: The "Illinois Award for Literature." . . .

Brooks: That is what Robert Cromie, a Council advisor at the time, formally named it. I think I startled them by suggesting that $10,000 would not be too much to give. Perhaps that may happen some day.

Angle: And this kind of thing you believe to be the best means of fostering writing?

Brooks: Certainly one of the best. For there aren't too many things you can do for a writer. The best thing you can do for a writer is to keep him from starving, and to provide some degree of free time for him.

Angle: I suppose you are right. Do you know of any state that is doing more along this line than Illinois?

Brooks: I don't know anything about this, but I keep hearing that New York is doing a good deal.

Angle: New York has a very active arts council, although it is young. Our Illinois Arts Council is young too, and it might be induced to branch out in such directions as you have suggested. I don't think I have asked you whether there were aspects of life in Chicago that you thought were unusually stimulating to a writer?

Brooks: We all know that the University of Chicago is a center of arts activities, but there are other centers here too. We have the Hull House Theatre, the Skyloft Players, and there are some very exciting things going on at Columbia College, the Communication Arts School. William Russo's Center for New Music is there, and there is a local repertory there—the Chicago Opera Theatre; and there is the new Story Workshop which has quite a reputation throughout the country. . . .

Angle: Can you tell me a little more about the Story Workshop?

Brooks: I have not attended it, but the persons who have feel that it has helped them develop new sensitivities to words; that they are learning much about themselves, as well as about things that may be done with language.

Angle: How is the Story Workshop reached?

Brooks: It is a regular course now offered by Columbia College, and the students. . . .

Angle: Enroll and pay a tuition fee?
Brooks: Yes.

Angle: And do you have to be registered in Columbia College to do that?
Brooks: I believe so, yes.

Angle: And if I were an aspiring writer, I couldn't just go and attend, even though I paid a fee?

Brooks: I believe that the students are favored because John Schultz does not want a large group—he wants to manage no more than sixteen during the extent of the course. Enthusiastic interest such as yours, however, might induce Mirron Alexandroff, Columbia's president, to try extending this operation.

Angle: I should like to ask you what may be my final question. You have already answered it but I would like to emphasize it again. For the awakened writer, or one who has some awareness of capacity in this field, the most important thing that he or she can do by way of preparation is to get as much of an education as possible. Am I right in that?

Brooks: I feel that a writer should get as much education as possible, but just going to school is not enough; if it were, all owners of doctorates would be inspired writers. But you and I know that many a Dr. Puffanblow writes a duller piece than does Susie Butterball, the high school sophomore. A writer needs to read almost more than his eyes can bear, to know what is going on, and what *has gone on*, not only in his own field but in related fields. And a writer needs general knowledge. And a writer needs to write. And a writer needs to live richly with eyes open, and heart, too.

Angle: Is there anything that you would like to say further that we haven't touched on?

Brooks: Well, here are answers to questions I am often asked. 1. What is the significance of the Pulitzer Prize? I would say that it is a pleasant salute. It is a smile, usually accepted. 2. Why do you write poetry? I like the concentration, the crush; I like working with language, as others like working with paints and clay, or notes. 3. Has much of your poetry a racial element? Yes. It is organic, not imposed. It is my privilege to state "Negroes" not as curios but as people. 4. What is your Poet's Premise? "Vivify the contemporary fact," said Whitman. I like to vivify the *universal* fact, when it occurs to me. But the universal wears contemporary clothing very well.

Gwendolyn Brooks

Roy Newquist / 1967

From *Conversations* by Roy Newquist (Chicago: Rand McNally & Company, 1967): 36–46.

Brooks: I was born in Topeka, Kansas, on June 7, 1917. I've always resented that fact because my parents were living in Chicago, but my mother wanted me to be born in her home town, with her mother, so when I was due to arrive she went to Topeka. When I was about a month old we came back to Chicago, so I feel that I'm really a native Chicagoan. After all, I grew up here and attended Chicago public schools.

I started writing poetry—according to my mother—when I was about seven years old. At least, I tried to put rhymes together. I don't have any poems on hand that go back quite that far, but I do have some that date to the age of eleven. In fact, I have many old notebooks filled with poems that I'll show to nobody, except to family members occasionally, when they want to have a good laugh.

We had many books in the house, always, and I was blessed with a very encouraging mother and father. My father used to tell stories to my brother and myself and sing us old songs and read us old poems.

My parents did nothing professional as far as the arts were concerned. My father brought home books and music because he worked at the McKinley Music Publishing Company. They were very fond of him (he was a shipping clerk) and they would give him music and old books. He died in 1959. My mother always wanted to be a pianist; she plays very nicely, to entertain herself, and about twenty years ago she began to compose music. She took a course I harmony at one of the evening schools, then started to compose, though she never attempted anything on a professional basis.

When I was eleven I started to get *Writer's Digest*. I don't know how I saw it; I wasn't in the habit of going to the downtown bookstores. I read a lot; we had the *Harvard Classics* at home, and there was a good library at the Forrestville Public School two blocks away. And I wrote, but I didn't sell anything. I believe I did place some poems in those anthologies that require you to buy a number of copies in exchange for the honor of being published.

I saw my first published poem in *American Childhood* magazine; the pay was six copies of that issue. During my sixteenth and seventeenth years I had seventy-five poems printed in the *Chicago Defender*, in the "Lights and Shadows" column which they no longer have. Aside from these pleasantries I didn't publish a poem in a well-known magazine until I was twenty-eight, even though I had sent poems to poetry magazines for fourteen years. Finally *Poetry* magazine published a group of four. This should encourage youngsters who feel discouraged at not getting anything published. All you have to do is stick it out for fourteen years. I thank the editors, now, for not publishing the first things I sent in. I would have been thoroughly ashamed of them. That, too, should be a lesson to the young.

My last two years of high school were spent at Englewood. There I met a history teacher, Miss Hern, a very strict teacher who paid no attention to me until I did a history report. The report was on a historical title titled *Janice West*. I hated the book, and in order to make things a little more bearable for myself I wrote the report in rhyme. Miss Hern was fascinated at the idea of someone trying to do such a thing. She became interested in me and told me that someday I might become a poet.

Also at Englewood I had a journalism teacher named Margaret Anderson. I've been trying to find her for lo, these many years, because she was very encouraging to me. She took time to talk to me, to ask me about my family, whether there were writers in the family, where I got my ideas. And a Horace Williston encouraged me in writing; aside from these three teachers I can't remember anyone outside of my family giving me any encouragement at all. Things were not then as they are now; today so much stress is given to creative writing, to school newspapers and magazines.

I did have some negative experiences. When I was going to Forrestville Elementary School I used to write compositions, and my English teachers were rather skeptical of them. Finally one of them sent a note to my mother, telling her that I was plagiarizing, stealing the works of published writers and using them as compositions. My mother flew to the school and insulted the teacher. She said that my English was better than hers, that I certainly had not plagiarized anything, that everything I turned in was my own work, and that I would sit right there and write something comparable if the teacher wanted me to. The teacher had me do something on that order, then admitted that she guessed I hadn't plagiarized.

From the beginning my mother told me and everybody else that I would be a second Paul Laurence Dunbar. She was positive that my future depended only upon time; time would take care of everything, and I would be published. She had more faith in me than I did. I was convinced I would never be published, and from time to time I would bury the poems I wrote in the back yard to be dug up in the future, the way they do time capsules now. I must have written at least a thousand lousy poems and buried them.

I did show a little enterprise. When I was thirteen I founded a newspaper titled *The Champlain Weekly News*. My mother helped me make copies of the paper, and I sold it to the neighbors for a nickel apiece. It got so that the neighbors were very eager for the weekly news to arrive. Some people rather took me to task because I would listen very eagerly to the neighborhood gossip. My mother wasn't much of a gossip, but she has a good receiver, and the women in the neighborhood loved to tell her their troubles and their tragedies, and I would "accidentally" overhear them. We rented out an apartment upstairs, and I would stand in the vestibule listening to all the life that went on up there. I think everyone was greatly relieved when I gave up my career as newspaperwoman.

I really haven't had an exciting life. I went to Wilson Junior College, and when I graduated I went to Illinois State Employment Service and applied for a job. They gave me a most peculiar one. (So peculiar and memorable that the book I'm writing now, a full-length poem, is based upon it.) They sent me to the Mecca Building—the address was 3838 South State Street—and I was to be a secretary to a Dr. E. N. French, who turned out to be a spiritual advisor. He had a storefront and four secretaries, all of whom were kept busy answering letters, taking the money out of the envelopes, and giving it to him. He would mail the people who sent in money anything they asked for—holy thunderbolts, charms, dusts of different kinds, love potions, heaven knows what all. The secretaries were also expected to help make up some of these charms. He had a regular little bottling operation. Some of his clientele lived or worked in the Mecca Building, and I delivered potions and charms and got to know some of these people. Oh, it was a bleak condition of life.

This was in October of 1936, and I stayed with Dr. French for the most horrible four months of my existence. I still recall vividly how I suffered. But it was my first job, and I hated to go home a failure. Besides, it was depression time, and my father was always poorly paid, so the small amount of money I got ($8.00 a week) was quite a bit for a job of that sort in those lean days. The money helped at home—I can remember my mother being able to buy draperies for the house—so I hated to quit. I stayed until Dr. French informed me that, because he thought I could speak well, he would employ me as his assistant pastor in the church he operated next door. A storefront church, naturally.

Dr. French was the most awesome West Indian; he wore a little black cap, and he was extremely fierce and stern. But I did have enough sense to tell him that I certainly was not going to become an assistant pastor. He said, "You will, or you'll leave. Don't come back to work Monday if you fail to show up Sunday at the church." I didn't show up Sunday, but I did go back to work Monday because I didn't think he meant his threat. Besides, he owed me money. But he told me I was fired, and I didn't get my last money earned, but at least I got out of there and went home from that horrible place for the last time.

After that I joined the NAACP Youth Council. A couple of girl friends asked me to join it because there was so much liveliness going on, dances and things. And it was there that I met my husband. He had been sent by a mutual girl friend of ours, who said that since he was writing poetry, he should join this council to meet a girl who was writing poetry, too. So I was sitting with her, and this glorious man appeared in the doorway and posed for a moment, looking the situation over, and I said, "There is the man I'm going to marry." It seems remarkably bold of me, perhaps farsighted in a blind sort of way. I was always impressed by dignity in a man, and he certainly had that. So my girl friend, having spunk and fire, said, "Hey, boy, this girl wants to meet you." And I met him.

I became publicity director for the NAACP Youth Council, and I was deeply impressed with some of the things these young people were doing. It also turned out to be the first time I was really accepted by people of my own age. You see, the children I went to school with and the people in my neighborhood were not interested in the things I was concerned with. I liked to read, and everyone else considered reading a chore. And I liked to draw, as my brother did. I played the piano a bit, and all these things combined to make me seem a rather strange individual. In the Youth Council, however, I met people who were artists, good pianists, writers. Many of them have become very successful. Johnny Johnson (now head of the Johnson Publishing Company) was there when I was, and John Karl, a very famous artist in San Francisco. So for the first time I found myself accepted by the young of my own approximate age, and it was very exciting, and I stayed with it for a while after I was married.

I got married in September of 1939, and my son was born in October 1940; after that I was too busy to run around to meetings. But in 1941 Inez Cun-

ningham Stark—a reader for *Poetry* magazine and an eccentric society ma-
tron (it doesn't seem right, somehow, to call her that, but none of us who
knew her could forget her fantastic John Fredericks hats) decided that she
would like to come to the South Side Community Arts Center, which was
still at 38th and Michigan, and start a new poetry group for the southsiders.
This must have been the most exciting thing that had happened to me because
she introduced me to modern poetry.

I had already been introduced to modern poetry, in a sense, when I was
sixteen. I had written to James Weldon Johnson, who wrote *God's Trombones*, asking him to look at some of the poems I was enclosing and tell me
what he thought of them. He wrote back and told me that he saw some hope,
but that what I needed to do was to read a great deal of modern poetry. Not
to imitate it, but to absorb it, to know what people of the present day were
doing. He suspected that I was a subscriber to Wordsworth, Coleridge, and
Keats, all of whom were excellent poets and still have much to give, but that
I knew nothing about Eliot or [John Crowe] Ransom or Frost, or the other
contemporary poets I should have been reading. I regret to this day that I
didn't read modern poetry and fiction and philosophy when I was extremely
young. It wasn't my parents' fault; they had the books at hand, standing
firmly in the bookcase in the dining room. I would go and open up the glass
doors of that bookcase and take out fairy tales and simpler things. Foolishly
I let the books that contained the moderns just stand there.

We read modern poetry in this group, and Mrs. Stark had very little to say.
She would start the ball rolling and we would do the rest, lighting into each
other's poems with great spirit. It is the only poetry group I ever encountered
where people really told each other what they thought; they didn't care how
feelings got hurt. Many a young woman went home crying; many a young
man went home mad. It was very helpful. Oddly enough, Margaret Danner
was the worst writer in the group. Everyone used to laugh at her. No one
thought she would ever do anything. She really started from the bottom, but
she grew to be, for a while, an assistant editor of *Poetry* magazine when Karl
Shapiro was there. She went to Detroit and opened a salon, but I understand
she's back in Chicago, and she's one of our really good poets. There were so
many good poets in that group, most of whom have stopped writing. Margaret
Walker came a few times; she's just published a novel titled *Jubilee*.

Many of the poems contained in my first book were written when I was in
that group. This was 1941, 1942. Then many of the men were sent away to
war, and a few of them were killed. I suppose, in a way, an age had ended.

The next thing that happened of significance—speaking in the literary sense—was when I spotted a notice in one of the Chicago newspapers which announced that the Midwestern Writers' Conference was sponsoring a poetry contest, and that manuscripts should be sent to the Cordin Club at 410 South Michigan. So I sent some of my poems in. Then, out of the blue, Alice Manning Dickie, who used to be an editor for *Woman's Home Companion*, came over to see me one Saturday morning. She had to climb a long flight of stairs to one of the kitchenette apartments I had not only lived in, but had written so much about, and she said that she was shocked to discover that I was a Negro. She must have begun to suspect it when she entered the neighborhood. (We were living at 623 East Sixty-third Street then.) She wanted to know how in the world I had heard of the Midwestern Writers' Contest, and I told her I had seen it in the paper.

The poem had won first prize. The next year I entered and won first prize again. The third year the Midwestern Writers' Conference was combined with what was called the Annual Writers' Conference and held on the North-western University campus. Paul Engle was teaching a summer course out there, and he became very interested in the work I was doing. Perhaps this was because he was so unimpressed with the work others were doing. At any rate, he said it was a relief to find something worthwhile.

In the contest they had that year I won first prize, and that, Pulitzer Prize notwithstanding, is the prize that has meant the most to me, personally. So much was attendant upon it.

The awards ceremony was held at Cahn Auditorium, and the hall was flooded with people. No one expected a little Negro girl to win a prize, and when Paul Engle called my name I just sat there. I didn't expect to win, either. I had thought of how nice it would be to win the poetry prize again, but I didn't think I would. So I sat there, finding it hard to believe that he was really calling my name, wanting me to come up to the stage to get the first prize. When it seemed that I wasn't going to get up at all, Paul Engle said, "You'd better come up here, Gwendolyn, or I'll give the prize to someone else."

Finally I walked up there. I'll never forget the gasps that went through the audience. Remember, things were different then, and Negroes just didn't win prizes of that sort. But poetry doesn't exactly earn a living, you know—it didn't then, it doesn't now—and at that time I was primarily a housewife, which is the last thing I'm really interested in being. I was at home all the time. I enjoyed my son, even though I was a nervous wreck when I was a mother for the first time; I didn't understand anything about children, and he was an experiment. I think he rather senses that. I enjoyed bringing up my daughter more because I knew a bit more of what to do, what to expect.

In 1944 I sent a collection of poems, nineteen in all, to Harper because I decided it was time to try to get a book published. I had met Emily Morrison at the first Midwestern Writers' Conference, and she told me that when I had enough poems to make a book, she would like to see them. So I sent all these verses that had no connection, really, but she was canny enough to see a connection in several of the poems, those that dealt with Negroes. She said that was my forte, not to write disconnectedly about such things as love, death, and the mysteries of life, but to center my ideas in the background I really knew something about. She thought the best of those poems dealt with Negroes, so I took her word and gathered them together and called the collection *A Street in Bronzeville*. My idea was to take my own street and write about a person or incident associated with each of the houses on the block.

Elizabeth Lawrence at Harper replied that indeed they were interested in bringing out a book of my poems and to take my time. But I couldn't take my time, so I sat down immediately and wrote a long poem and a series of war sonnets. With her letter, incidentally, she sent a copy of a letter from Richard Wright, to whom they had shown the manuscript. He was enthusiastic, but he didn't care for my title. He said no one would understand what "Bronzeville" meant, and it turned out that he was right. Negroes and whites alike are forever asking me what it means. It refers to what used to be, and really is still, the largest Negro area in Chicago. In those days it was very well defined; I know. There was not one Negro east of Cottage Grove Avenue. I used to take my little boy over there on walks, and we counted ourselves lucky when we weren't thrown at.

I wrote those extra poems and they said I'd done enough and that they would bring out the book. It took nine months. It was published on VJ-Day in August 1945, and attracted a great deal of attention. It wasn't too hard to attract attention with a book in those days; soldiers were reading madly, and books sold well, even poetry. My book had a rather folksy narrative nature, and I guess that is one way to get poetry in front of people: to tell stories. Everyone loves stories, and a surprising number of people can be trapped into a book of verse if there's a promise of a story. The legend on the cover of the book, "Ballads and blues . . ." promised excitement.

I suppose the next truly big thing that happened to me was being awarded the Pulitzer Prize for Poetry in 1950. It still seems like a thing that couldn't have happened to me. And it came, you might say, out of the blue.

One day a reporter from the *Chicago Sun-Times* called me and said, "Do you know that you have won the Pulitzer Prize?" I screamed and said something about not believing it. I was stunned. I grabbed my little boy (he was nine at the time); we had been getting ready to go to the movies. Anything was better than sitting home in the dark. We'd had our lights turned off because we hadn't paid the bill; we were very poor. So we went to the movies, but I don't' think I saw or heard a thing; I kept believing and not believing I'd won the Pulitzer Prize.

The next day was exciting and a little appalling at the same time. Newspaper reporters and photographers came out, most of them in the daytime, which wasn't too bad. But the *Chicago Tribune* came out at twilight, and they were going to take pictures and would need electricity. I sat there frozen. (I wonder if other people who think of themselves as being sensible do such foolish things.) I sat, waiting in a sort of quiet terror for him to put the plug into the socket. Then came that horrible moment when he put it in, and strangely enough, the lights came on. I still don't know how this happened. My husband said he had done something abut the light situation but that they couldn't have turned them on that quickly. So that's the story of the Pulitzer Prize. Light in darkness.

I mentioned before that one does not make a living from poetry, and that is so sadly true. This is one reason why I've taught for many years—perhaps the better way of putting it would be to say that I've led classes. I don't consider myself a teacher. I don't have teacher's training or certificates, and I'm sure that I've been accepted in schools because my Pulitzer Prize represents a diploma of some sort.

The first person who showed an interest in having me do this sort of work—helping? Lightly leading? Surely not teaching!—was Mike [Norman] Alexandrof, the president of Columbia College here in Chicago, a communication arts school. He told me he wanted me to conduct a poetry workshop to encourage young people to write. The first classes were in the evening, so I had people of all ages, not just young people. I had one sprightly little woman in her sixties who wanted to write poetry so badly; I saw her a few months ago, and she has been publishing poetry in various magazines and seemed very happy about it.

In these classes I play records—*The Waste Land, Spoon River Anthology*, Robert Frost, and many other modern poets—Dylan Thomas, Marianne

Moore. Then we have panel discussions and debates, and I stress that they must read and read and read and write and write and write. They always seem to be very interested.

I think that the beat poets have had something to do with the interest young people have in poetry. What the beats had to say, while certainly not in the kind of verse I would want to write, related to them, to our world. When I have them write beat poetry as an exercise I tell them, "You will probably never want to write another beat poem, but it's a wonderful muscle-loosening exercise." The beat poets seem to have invested modern poetry with some fresh air and blood it really needed.

The people in the workshops have told me, over and over again, that they had hated poetry because they were forced to memorize it in elementary school and high school, and it was presented to them as something heavy, to be gotten through for the sake of grades. The thing I am interested in doing is in presenting poetry as a living thing, an instrument of pleasure, of release, and they enjoy it when it's given to them that way. I make them write a lot, and once in a while they'll groan about that. Each student must write a book of twenty or twenty-five poems, depending upon the time we have. The few sessions when I've taught a fiction workshop I have them write groups of stories or short novels. My motto could be: "It's all in the doing."

The gratifying thing is that I find a great deal of talent, real talent. I've found people I envy, turning out very good poetry and very good fiction. Most of them are willing to work very hard. There are a few, always, who come there just for the grades, and I try to impress upon them that grades are of little interest to me. I regret the fact that I have to give them. But I have been amazed at the willingness of students, young and old, to put real energy and time and thought into their projects. I know how much *is* put in because I have to read their works and comment on them. And I must comment on every page submitted, because if I leave one unscrawled-upon it's brought to me and I'm asked, "What did you think about this? You didn't write anything, so I'm wondering if you thought it was so bad there was nothing to say."

Teaching, readings, being a mother to a teen-age daughter, and a wife to a fine and talented husband—these things take up time, and the time is well-spent. But I'm still primarily a poet, a necessary and perhaps compulsive thing. And I think that my poetry is related to life in the broad sense of the word, even though the subject matter relates closest to the Negro. Although I have called my first book, *A Street in Bronzeville,* I hoped that people would recognize instantly that Negroes are just like other people; they have the same hates and loves and fears, the same tragedies and triumphs and deaths, as people of any race or religion or nationality. I did not start writing to be a propagandist. I began writing because I love to write, and wrote about whatever I thought I thought. As I grew older, of course, I realized that it was Negroes that I saw, so I wrote about Negroes.

But take a poem from *Bronzeville*, "The Preacher." It could be about any preacher ruminating behind the sermons, wondering how God is, what He thinks up there, alone. He wouldn't have to be black or brown or yellow or white to wonder about that. A poem like "The Kitchenette Building" applies more to Negroes, perhaps, because more Negroes live in kitchenette apartments than the members of other races because they are so cheap and, consequently, so bleak. I've lived in many of them, and wrote from my own experience. But I hope that people can come out of my books feeling, "Well, Negroes are people after all, despite how strange they look with that peculiar color." People still indulge in this feeling; they find what they don't know to be mysterious, and distrust it.

I feel the civil rights movement to be most important, naturally; I belong to the NAACP, contribute what I can afford to give them, and I've given to SNCC. They are young people who are fighting the battle for some of us older ones. I intend to continue to contribute as much as my income will allow. But I'm not active in a speaking or marching sense. I guess I'm too withdrawn.

My primary obligation as a person and a writer is to my poetry, to myself. The poetry is myself. When I sit down to write a poem it's because I've had an impression, an idea, an emotion. I feel something, and I want to put that something on paper. You might say, "Well, because you put it on paper you are obviously trying to interest other people." That is certainly true, but my first commitment is to getting myself onto the paper. Then I hope, naturally, that many, many people will want to read it.

Many writers do feel an urge to save the world, of course, and perhaps some of them have succeeded to some degree. When I was a little girl I felt that I might write something that would have great influence upon the world, but since I came to my senses I have not felt obliged to revolutionize the world in any way. Some things that I have written might sound otherwise, but my first idea is always to put what I thought and felt on paper. I wrote about the Emmett Till murder because it got to me. I was appalled like every civilized being was appalled. I was especially touched because my son was fourteen at the time, and I couldn't help but think that it could have been him down there if I'd sent him to Mississippi. That was a very personal expression. I tried to imagine how the young woman, the one who was whistled at, felt after the murder and after the trial, after her sight of the boy's mother. What it was like to live with a man who had spilled blood. I imagined that she would have certain cringing feelings when he touched her—at least I know I would.

Now I'm working on the long poem, the book-length poem titled, *In the Mecca*, based on my first job experience I mentioned before. So I guess that virtually everything I write comes from life, and must come from life, to have validity.

This is an exciting age to be writing in. I think that the present great interest in form and language was bound to happen, if only as a reaction to the dull sleepiness of the preceding years. I don't think that the present intense concentration on very close, very textured language will last. I think that poets and readers will soon become interested again in presenting life in all its rich and diverse aspects. But I also think the good writing will continue without being as specialized and finicky as it is today. I guess I'm part of the persuasion; I too love to fight with a line or with a phrase. But I think most of the writers, the good writers, will become less self-conscious as time goes on. After all, the important emotions and subjects and ideas are made more exciting through clarity, and the way to that admirable combination of reality and power stand out in Dylan Thomas and T. S. Eliot and Yevtushenko, and are now most enthusiastically found in Voznesensky. Voznesensky seems to be so much a part of today in both language and subject; I think he's a good forerunner of what we may expect from the future.

An Interview with Gwendolyn Brooks

George Stavros / 1969

From *Contemporary Literature* 11, no. 1 (Winter 1970), 1–20. Reprinted by permission of the University of Wisconsin Press.

Q. You've written in the poem "The Chicago Picasso," which appears in your latest book, *In the Mecca*, that "we must cook ourselves and style ourselves for Art, who / is a requiring courtesan." And in an earlier poem, "The Egg Boiler," the speaker says that the poet creates his poems "out of air . . . And sometimes weightlessness is much to bear." Let me ask you to comment on these passages. Are they fair statements of your feelings about art and the position of the poet?

A. Well, in "The Chicago Picasso," first of all I was asked to write a poem by the mayor of Chicago about that statue, and I hadn't seen it. I had only seen pictures of it, and the pictures looked very foolish, with those two little eyes and the long nose. And I don't know a great deal about art myself; I haven't studied it. So I really didn't feel qualified to discuss what Picasso was doing or had intended to do. So I decided to handle the situation from the standpoint of how most of us who are not art fanciers or well educated in things artistic respond to just the word "art" and to its manifestations. And I decided that most of us do not feel cozy with art, that it's not a thing you easily and chummily throw your arms around, that it's not a huggable thing, as I said here: "Does man love Art? Man visits Art. . . ." And we visit it, we pay special, nice, precise little calls on it. But those of us who have not grown up with or to it perhaps squirm a little in its presence. We feel that something is required of us that perhaps we aren't altogether able to give. And it's just a way of saying, "Art hurts." Art is not an old shoe; it's something that you have to work in the presence of. It urges voyages. You just can't stay in your comfortable old grooves. You have to extend yourself. And it's easier to stay at home and drink beer.

Q. Were you satirizing those people who do stay at home and drink beer?

A. No. No, I'm not satirizing them, because I'm too close to them to do that. I "stay at home" (mostly) and drink Pepsi-Cola. I can't poke fun at them. But I do urge them—because after I saw the Picasso I admired it, and I'm glad it's in Chicago—I do ask them to look at that statue or any other piece of art that might seem perplexing and consider it as we might consider flowers. We don't ask a flower to give us any special reasons for its existence. We look at it and we are able to accept it as being something different, and different from ourselves. Who can explain a flower? But there it is. . . .

Q. I wonder if what you're saying applies to the poet or what poetry is? Is poetry like a flower that one must look at and perhaps not explain but just accept because it is there?

A. I think a little more should be required of the poet than perhaps is required of the sculptor or the painter. The poet deals in words with which everyone is familiar. We all handle words. And I think the poet, if he wants to speak to anyone, is constrained to do something with those words so that they will (I hate to use the word) mean something, will be something that a reader may touch.

Q. Let me quote a passage from a statement you made in 1950 and see whether you think it is still valid.

A. Almost certainly not.

Q. You wrote, "But no real artist is going to be content with offering raw materials. The Negro poet's most urgent duty, at present, is to polish his technique, his way of presenting his truths and his beauties, that these may be more insinuating and, therefore, more overwhelming."[1]

A. I still do feel that a poet has a duty to words and that words can do wonderful things, and it's too bad to just let them lie there without doing anything with and for them. But let's see, I said something there about it being the Negro poet, and that's no longer the acceptable word; black is the word. [Reads:] "The Negro poet's most urgent duty, at present, is to polish his technique, his way of presenting his truths and his beauties. . . ."—1950. You know, the world has just turned over since then, and at that time I felt that most strongly, most strongly—I was very impatient with black poets who just put down anything off the tops of their heads and left it there. But something different is happening now. Black poets today—when I say black poets I mean something different from that old phrase "Negro poets"—black poets are becoming increasingly aware of themselves and their blackness, as

<hr />

[1] *Phylon*, XI (1950), 312.

they would say, are interested in speaking to black people, and especially do they want to reach those people who would never go into a bookstore and buy a $4.95 volume of poetry written by anyone. And I think this is very important, what they're doing. I didn't bring a new little book just off the press called *Don't Cry, Scream*, by Don Lee. Don Lee is an exception. He is changing all the time and is interested very much in what words can do, but there is also a brief to be put forward for those who are just very much excited about what is going on today and are determined to get that rich life and urgency down on paper. And I don't think we can turn our backs on those people and say airily, "That is not good poetry," because for one thing the whole concept of what "good poetry" is is changing today, thank goodness. I think it's a very healthy thing.

Q. Would you feel then that technique and traditional form mean less to black poets writing today?

A. I think form should be considered after I speak about technique, because I believe that later on—who knows, ten years or twenty years from now—what I said back there in 1950 will again be justifiable; by then the rawness will have come to some maturation. Hopefully something will have been decided, and the poets will then have time to play more with their art.

Q. You mentioned Don Lee. Who else do you think is promising? I know you are very interested in encouraging the work of new poets.

A. Yes, there are some very interesting ones. James Cunningham, who is teaching, incidentally, at the University of Wisconsin-Milwaukee, is very good and desperately improving himself. Etheridge Knight. Walter Bradford (*Poems from Prison*) is another comer in this thing; Don Lee, whom I've mentioned. Carolyn Rodgers has put out one little book very much respected by the younger poets, those who know her, and is about to bring out another one. Jewel Latimore is about to bring out a third little book. Ebon Dooley. These are people who are very well known in Chicago, and their poetry is almost adored. I went to a reading of a little group of poets just a couple of weeks ago in the Affro-Arts Theater in Chicago, and it was packed with young people chiefly, who had come to hear poetry. This was unheard of a few years ago.

Q. How about poets who are more widely known? How do you fit LeRoi Jones among these writers?

A. Oh, he is their hero! He's their semi-model, the one they worship. I personally feel that he is one of the very good poets of today, and people hearing this who have no real knowledge of his work, but have just seen a couple of "inflammatory" passages in the newspapers, might say, "Well, what in the world do you mean? That's no poet." But he is a most talented person. His work *works*.

Q. What do you feel makes Jones's the voice of his generation?

A. Well, first of all he speaks to black people. They appreciate that. And he's uncompromising in his belief that the black people must subscribe to black solidarity and black self-consciousness.

Q. Is it his message or a poetic method that makes his poetry appeal particularly to blacks?

A. If it is a "method," it comes just from the sincere interest in his own people and in his desire to reach them, to speak to them of what he believes is right.

Q. Is he employing any traditional forms, would you say, that may be associated with blacks, say, jazz rhythms. . . ?

A. Yes, he and a number of the other black poets such as Larry Neal are interested in supplying black poetry with some strains of black music which they feel is the true art of the black people. They worship Coltranc and Ornette Coleman, and whenever they can they try to push such music into their work. Sometimes the poetry seems to grow out of the music.

Q. You've said that poetry is an entirely different thing now from what it was twenty years ago. Do you feel, as some readers of yours have said, that your own poetry has abandoned its lyrical simplicity for an angrier, more polemical public voice?

A. Those are the things that people say who have absolutely no understanding of what's going on and no desire to understand. No, I have not abandoned beauty, or lyricism, and I certainly don't consider myself a polemical poet. I'm just a black poet, and I write about what I see, what interests me, and I'm seeing new things. Many things that I'm seeing now I was absolutely blind to before, but I don't sit down at the table and say, "Lyricism is out." No, I just continue to write about what confronts me. . . . I get an idea or an impression or I become very excited about something and I can hardly wait till the time comes when I can get to the paper. In the meantime I take notes, little bits of the idea I put down on paper, and when I'm ready to write I write as urgently and directly as I possibly can. And I don't go back to mythology or my little textbooks. I know about the textbooks, but I'm not concerned with them during the act of poetry-writing.

Q. In one of the "Sermons on the Warpland," you quote Ron Karenga to the effect that blackness "is our ultimate reality."
A. I firmly believe it.

Q. Then am I right in saying these "Sermons" are almost apocalyptic or prophetic? They seem rather. . . .
A. They're little addresses to black people, that's all.

Q. The last poem in the group ("The time / cracks into furious flower. . . .") suggests that there will be a rebirth.
A. Yes. . . . There's something I'd like to say about my intent as a poet that you touched upon a moment ago and which has some connection with that business of abandoning lyricism, et cetera. Changes in my work—there *is* something different that I want to do. I want to write poems that will be non-compromising. I don't want to stop a concern with words doing good jobs, which has always been a concern of mine, but I want to write poems that will be meaningful to those people I described a while ago, things that will touch them.

Let me tell you about an experience I had in Chicago. I went around with a few of those poets that I've just mentioned. They go to housing projects and out in the parks sometimes, and just start reading their poetry; and right around the corner—across the street from the Wall in Chicago, the Wall of Respect. . . .

Q. That's the one you write about in "The Wall."
A. Yes. Well, right across the street is a tavern, and one Sunday afternoon, some of the poets decided to go in there and read poetry to just whoever was there. I went with them. One of them went to the front of the tavern and said, "Say, folks, we're going to lay some poetry on you." And there had been a couple of fights in there, people drinking, and all kinds of exciting things going on; and some of us wondered how they were going to respond to poetry. But the poets started reading their poetry, and before we knew it, people had turned around on their bar stools, with their drinks behind them, and were listening. Then they applauded. And I thought that was a wonderful thing, something new to me. I want to write poetry—and it won't be Ezra Pound poetry, as you can imagine—that will be exciting to such people. And I don't see why it can't be "good" poetry, putting quotes around "good."

Q. Are you suggesting that poetry should be restored to one of its original forms, that of the voice of the prophet, speaker to the people . . . ?

A. I don't want to be a prophet.

Q. . . . Or a social voice, a voice that can be heard. Do you think that poetry as it's now being written and heard by the people is becoming a social force?

A. Some of these people do want their poems to become "social forces"; others haven't, I believe, really thought of such a thing. And I am not writing poems with the idea that they are to become social forces. I don't feel that I care to direct myself in that way. I don't care to proceed from that intention.

Q. Let me ask you about the character portraits in your poetry and in your novel, *Maud Martha*. *In the Mecca*, your most recent volume, portrays life in a large city apartment building. *A Street in Bronzeville* gave similar vignettes of people in the city. The same, I think, can be said for all of your work.

A. It's a fascination of mine to write about ghetto people there.

Q. Are your characters literally true to your experience or do you set out to change experience?

A. Some of them are, are invented, some of them are very real people. The people in a little poem called "The Vacant Lot" really existed and really did those things. For example: "Mrs. Coley's three-flat brick / Isn't here any more. / All done with seeing her fat little form / Burst out of the basement door. . . ." Really happened! That lot is still vacant on the street where I was raised. (My mother still lives on the street.) "Matthew Cole" is based on a man who roomed with my husband's aunt. And I remember him so well, I feel he really came through in the poem. "The Murder" really happened except for the fact that I said the boy's mother was gossiping down the street. She was working. (I guess I did her an injustice there.) "Obituary for a Living Lady" is based on a person I once knew very well.

Q. What about the characters in *Maud Martha*? I'm thinking of Clement Lewy, a boy who comes home every day to prepare his own meal while his mother is at work. Or the character of the young truck driver who finds that he cannot any longer abide his home life and one day simply abandons his family.

A. Again, not based on any specific persons.

Q. There is a quality of pathos about all of your characters and compassion in your treatment of them. Many of them make a pitiful attempt to be what they cannot be.

A. Some of them. Not all of them; some of them are very much interested in just the general events of their own lives.

Q. Let me suggest one of the frequently anthologized poems, "A Song in the Front Yard," about a girl who "gets sick of a rose" and decides she'd like to leave the comfort and pleasure of the front yard to see what life would be like in the back.

A. Or out in the alley, where the charity children play, based on my own resentment when I was a little girl, having to come inside the front gate after nine—oh, earlier than that in my case.

Q. Isn't there a yearning to get away in many such portraits?

A. I wouldn't attach any heavy significance to that particular poem, because that was the lightest kind of a little poem.

Q. How about a poem like "Sadie and Maud," a little lyric, I think in quatrains, contrasting Maud, who turns out to be a lonely brown "mouse," and Sadie, who "scraped life / With a fine tooth comb"?

A. Those are imaginary characters, purely imaginary.

Q. What about "The Sundays of Satin-Legs Smith," where the hero spends much of his morning in his lavender bath. . . .

A. . . . and in his closet, among his perfume bottles.

Q. And his neckties and umbrellas which are like "banners for some gathering war"?

A. Not his umbrellas; I think I called it hats "like bright umbrellas," which implies that he is protecting himself under that fancy wideness. . . . You probably don't remember the zoot-suiters; they were still around in the forties, in the early forties. They were not only black men but Puerto Ricans, too, who would wear these suits with the wide shoulders, and the pants did balloon out and then come down to tapering ends, and they wore chains— perhaps you've seen them in the movies every once in a while. That's the kind of person I was writing about in "The Sundays of Satin-Legs Smith."

Q. You write about young men in other poems perhaps like that. "Patent Leather" was an early poem describing a character who talks about his "cool chick down on Calumet," and he wears patent leather. Then there's "Bronzeville Man with a Belt in the Back," and more recently, "We Real Cool."

A. In "Patent Leather," a young woman is admiring a man (and that admiration is no longer popular) who slicks back his hair, so that it looks like it's smooth as patent leather, and shiny. "Bronzeville Man with a Belt in the Back"—"belt in the back" was a popular style for men some years ago; and this man feels dapper and equal to the fight that he must constantly wage, when he puts on such a suit.

Q. How about the seven pool players in the poem "We Real Cool"?

A. They have no pretensions to any glamor. They are supposedly drop-outs, or at least they're in the poolroom when they should possibly be in school, since they're probably young enough, or at least those I saw were when I looked in a poolroom, and they. . . . First of all, let me tell you how that's supposed to be said, because there's a reason why I set it out as I did. These are people who are essentially saying, "Kilroy is here. We are." But they're a little uncertain of the strength of their identity. [Reads: "We Real Cool."]

The "We"—you're supposed to stop after the "We" and think about their validity, and of course there's no way for you to tell whether it should be said softly or not, I suppose, but I say it rather softly because I want to represent their basic uncertainty, which they don't bother to question every day, of course.

Q. Are you saying that the form of this poem, then, was determined by the colloquial rhythm you were trying to catch?

A. No, determined by my feeling about these boys, these young men.

Q. These short lines, then, are your own invention at this point? You don't have any literary model in mind; you're not thinking of Eliot or Pound or anybody in particular . . . ?

A. My gosh, no! I don't even admire Pound, but I do like, for instance, Eliot's "Prufrock" and *The Waste Land*, "Portrait of a Lady," and some others of those earlier poems. But nothing of the sort ever entered my mind. When I start writing a poem, I don't think about models or about what any-body else in the world has done.

Q. Let me ask you about some of your poems that are in specific forms, however—sonnets. . . .

A. I like to refer to that series of soldier sonnets.

Q. "Gay Chaps at the Bar."

A. A sonnet series in off-rhyme, because I felt it was an off-rhyme situa-tion—I did think of that. I first wrote the one sonnet, without thinking of extensions. I wrote it because of a letter I got from a soldier who included that title in what he was telling me; and then I said, there are other things to say about what's going on at the front and all, and I'll write more poems, some of them based on the stuff of letters that I was getting from several soldiers, and I felt it would be good to have them all in the same form, because it would serve my purposes throughout.

Q. Then you find it challenging to write in a particular form, like the sonnet, when the occasion seems to lend itself?

A. I really haven't written extensively in many forms. I've written a little blank verse, and I have written many more sonnets than I'm sure I'll be writing in the future, although I still think there are things colloquial and contemporary that can be done with the sonnet form. And, let's see, free verse of course I'll be continuing to experiment with, dotting a little rhyme here and there sometimes as I did in part of *In the Mecca*. But I'm really not form-conscious. I don't worship villanelles, for instance.

Q. But then you have written formally, as you say, with sonnets, quatrains, the literary ballad, the folk ballad, "The Ballad of Rudolph Reed." Have you given up writing ballads?

A. I don't know. I might write other ballads, but they would be very different from those that I have written so far. I see myself chiefly writing free verse, experimenting with it as much as I can. The next book, I'm pretty sure, will be a book of small pieces of free verse.

Q. Do you consider the opening lines of *In the Mecca* as being typical of what you're trying to do in that poem? "Sit where the light corrupts your face. / Miës Van der Rohe retires from grace. / And the fair fables fall . . ."—and continuing. They're rather irregular free verse lines.

A. Sometimes I shall perhaps do something on that order. (You are, of course, speaking of the lines that follow those three.) But then I can't guarantee it. Suppose I thought of a poem that was free verse but didn't have such a variety of lengths of line; that would still be all right.

Q. A much-admired poem from *Annie Allen* is the one beginning "A light and diplomatic bird / Is lenient in my window tree. / A quick dilemma of the leaves / Discloses twist and tact to me." Do you feel this is representative of your lyrical expression?

A. No, I wouldn't say that this is a representative poem, a poem that represents my usual sort of expression. This is to be considered as part of the story of Annie Allen. She's unhappy here, and she's looking out of the window at a tree near the window, and she sees a little bird, and she envies this bird because, of course, who knows?, the bird might have been as miserable as she was; but for all that she can tell he is able to absorb his own grief, and she has a little fancy conceit here: she's saying that he's singing out of pity for her. "He can afford his sine die. / He can afford to pity me. . . ." Tell me how to be well balanced; tell me how to "bleach" (sic) away the impurities. It's really a very simple little thing that has no comparison, say, to a poem like "kitchenette building." I believe I have written more "kitchenette building"–type poems than I have written about birds singing and feeling sorry for a girl who's temporarily overwhelmed by grief.

Q. What was behind the title, "The Anniad," in the first place? Is this a classical reference?

A. Well, the girl's name was Annie, and it was my little pompous pleasure to raise her to a height that she probably did not have, and I thought of the *Iliad* and said, I'll call this "The Anniad." At first, interestingly enough, I called her Hester Allen, and I wanted then to say "The Hesteriad," but I forget why I changed it to Annie. . . . I was fascinated by what words might do there in the poem. You can tell that it's labored, a poem that's very interested in the mysteries and magic of technique.

Q. Technique—you've written, for example, seven-line stanzas. Is there any reason for that?

A. Lucky seven, I guess. I like the number seven. That really is probably not the reason; I really can't remember exactly, but I imagine I finished one stanza, then decided that the rest of them would be just like that.

Q. I think the seventh stanza is typical of not only the meter but the imagery and symbolism: "And a man of tan engages / For the springtime of her pride, / Eats the green by easy stages, / Nibbles at the root beneath / With intimidating teeth. / But no ravishment enrages. / No dominion is defied."

A. What a pleasure it was to write that poem!

Q. Was what you're trying to do in a stanza like that different from what you had done up until that time, and why was it such a pleasure? The writing in general seems to differ from the earlier writing because it is more cryptic, more compressed. Is there any sense in which you feel you were trying something totally new here in the poem?

A. No, not something new. I was just very conscious of every word; I wanted every phrase to be beautiful, and yet to contribute sanely to the whole, to the whole effect.

Q. Taking this as a typical stanza, you have indications of springtime again, growth—greenery, "nibbles at the root beneath"; I imagine this is the root of their love. . . .

A. Yes, you understand how the young man is courting her, and it's a—really, I could have said what I wanted to say in two lines, you know; I could have said, well, he came and he pursued her, but she was all ready for the outcome, in fact, eagerly awaiting it.

Q. I was just suggesting that the stanza seems closely and carefully textured.

A. Yes, and so was every stanza in that poem; every one was worked on and revised, tenderly cared for. More so than anything else I've written, and it is not a wild success; some of it just doesn't come off. But it was enjoyable.

Q. Can you tell me what you're doing next?

A. I'm very excited about what I'll be doing in the immediate future, and I'm retiring from teaching so that I can give my real attention to working with poetry. . . . I imagine the future poems will seem more like some of the poems in *A Street in Bronzeville*.

Q. Please go on.

A. They'll deal with people, that I know; and I won't be trying to prove something as I write. I want them to be pictures of black life as I see it today. This of course would include people who do not think they're thinking about the great fight that's going on.

Q. From what you say about how you want your poetry not to teach anything but to stand on its own. . . .

A. Well, I don't say that I don't want it to teach anything; I'd merely say that when I write it, I don't have preaching in mind.

Q. Perhaps you agree with Ellison and Baldwin, who have attacked Wright's use of the protest novel, and believe that the protest novel should be replaced by something less social. Ellison said that the novelist ought to write on "the full range of American Negro humanity."[2]

---

[2] *Shadow and Act*, quoted in Seymour L. Gross and John Edward Hardy, eds., *Images of the Negro in American Literature* (Chicago, 1966) p. 20.

A. No, I don't feel that way at all. I feel that the poet should write out of his own milieu. Now, I'm not "full-range" qualified, I less than some others perhaps, less than a poet like Margaret Walker, who knows much more than I do about everything. But I am in the black community; I see what's going on there. I talk with these people. I know how many of them feel. I am not in the banker's community. I'm not acquainted, that I know of, with any Wall Street high influences—people who run the country, as they say. So therefore I would not attempt to write about them. Perhaps Ralph Ellison is acquainted with every aspect of American life; I can merely say that I'm not, so therefore I can't write about America inclusively. But that's all right—I'm not sorry. You know, William Faulkner felt that if he just stayed with Yoknapatawpha County he was all right, and that in just concentrating on that single area— and that single multiplicity!—of life, that that would be "general" enough for his purposes.

I started out talking about Bronzeville, but Bronzeville's almost meaning- less by now, I suppose, since Bronzeville has spread and spread and spread all over. Bronzeville, incidentally, was not my own title. That was invented by the *Chicago Defender* long, long ago to refer to the then black area.

Q. Is it still called that?

A. Once in a while you'll see on a store "Bronzeville Tailor Shop" or something like that, but almost nobody talks about Bronzeville.

Q. It's not a term as specific as Harlem in New York City, for example.

A. No.

Q. I know you've been living in Chicago most of your life and consider yourself a Chicago native, so there's a great feeling of place in your poetry—in *Maud Martha*, too. Do you try to evoke place in your work?

A. No, I start with the people. For instance, Maud Martha goes to the Regal Theater, which is almost dead now, but had a great history in Chicago. She looks at the people; she looks at the star; she looks at the people coming out of the theater. But suffice it to say that I don't start with the landmarks.

Q. A number of your poems, too, reflect your family life, certainly your mother, and you have written poems about motherhood. "The Motherhood" is part of the "Annie Allen" series. It's extremely effective, I think. Do you feel that there is much of your experience as a mother which has gone into those poems?

A. Chiefly my experience, not my own mother's experience.

Q. Your own experience as a mother, yes. I'm thinking of poems such as those beginning "People who have no children can be hard" or "What shall I give my children? who are poor, / Who are adjudged the leastwise of the land, / . . . my sweetest lepers" or ". . . shall I prime my children, pray, to pray?"

A. Yes, all questions I would ask of myself. My mother certainly wouldn't ask such a question of herself, that last one. She feels firmly that you must pray, and that only good can come of it.

Q. What of religion in your poems? I noticed that two or three of your references to men of the church are at least uncomplimentary. For example, there's Prophet Williams in *In the Mecca*—a faith healer.

A. Yes, he was based on an actual man that I worked for in the Mecca building. Haven't I told that story? Well, when I was nineteen and had just gotten out of junior college, I went to the Illinois State Employment Service to get a job. They sent me to the Mecca building to a spiritual adviser, and he had a fantastic practice, very lucrative. He had us bottling medicine as well as answering letters. Not real medicine, but love charms and stuff like that he called it, and I delivered it through the building; that was my introduction to the Mecca building. You've probably heard of the Mecca. John Bartlow Martin has written about it.

Q. Let me ask you about your novel, now that we've raised that question. It's been described as poetic prose. What did you set out to do in writing *Maud Martha*?

A. Well, I wanted to give a picture of a girl growing up—a black girl growing up in Chicago, and of course much of it is wrenched from my own life and twisted, but about its being poetic in parts, I suppose that could hardly be avoided, if it is a thing to be avoided, because even in writing prose I find myself weighing the possibilities of every word just as I do in a poem. This was true when I used to write reviews, too.

Q. Did you have any form in mind? I'd like to know how you decided upon the form of the novel—the small chapters, about thirty-four of them, the small prose sections fitting together into something like a mosaic.

A. Well, I had first written a few tiny stories, and I felt that they would mesh, and I centered them and the others around one character. If there is a form I would say it was imposed, at least in the beginning, when I started with those segments, or vignettes.

Q. Would it then be fair to say that the unity of the novel is simply the central point of view of Maud Martha herself as she grows up?

A. Yes, certainly.

Q. Have you given any thought to writing another novel?

A. No, because I don't feel that that is my category. No.

Q. Have you given any thought to writing a play?

A. Yes, small verse plays that will not be acted at all, but will just be published as poems, really. That doesn't mean that I've begun them, but they're in my mind. I do want to do that someday.

Q. Do you feel that writing in this form will help you develop different themes?

A. Well, if I can be said to be "using themes," I believe that the small verse plays would concern themselves with those same themes. I see no reason why the form should dictate different subjects. No, I believe I'll go right on writing about black people as people, and not "polemically," either.

Q. I meant to suggest that perhaps a more explicit social theme than you're willing to impose upon your poetry could be presented in say, the drama. I'm thinking of the plays of Jones and Baldwin.

A. Well, that would depend, I believe, upon the climate of America—if it changes, well, we all have to respond to the changes; that's what black people are doing now.

Q. How do you feel about that climate in regard to what the black writer is doing now? Do you think his task is becoming easier, more difficult, more important?

A. I think it is the task or job or responsibility or pleasure or pride of any writer to respond to his climate. You write about what is in the world. I think I would be silly, and so would LeRoi Jones, to sit down now under the trees and write about the Victorian age, unless there's some special reference we could make to what's going on now.

Q. Then your poems about Malcolm X and Medgar Evers, for example, are part of a continuing interest in poetry that involved you with matters of the day. Is that correct?

A. No, I didn't involve myself with Medgar Evers's assassination—I merely reacted to it, and I described what he had done, the effects he had had on the assaulting elements of his society, and I ended, most beautifully, I thought: "People said that / he was holding clean globes in his hands."

Q. What did you mean when you said he had departed from "Old styles, old tempos, all the engagement of / the day—the sedate, the regulated fray. . ."?

A. [Reads:] ". . . the antique light, the Moral rose, old gusts, / tight whistlings from the past, the mothballs / in the Love at last our man forswore." He just up and decided he wasn't going to have anything else to do with the stale traditions of the past and the hindrances and restrictions that American response to horrors had been concerned with.

Q. In other words, an impatience with injustice and continuing oppression.

A. Yes, he decided he would just "have none" of it anymore and would do something about righting things for his people.

Q. In your poem "The Wall," which accompanies the other dedication, "The Chicago Picasso," you write about "legislatures / of ploy and scruple and practical gelatin." Can you explain what you meant by that?

A. [Reads:] "On Forty-third and Langley / black furnaces resent ancient / legislatures"—first of all, the "black furnaces" are the very excited people that were out there in the street that day, and they resented the restrictions and the injustices—legal injustices, too—that had been visited upon them through centuries, hence "ancient." "Ploy"; "scruple"; "practical gelatin"—*that* is the injustice of a gelatinous nature that we are exposed to and for which we are told, in effect, that this is just something that has to be: "You can see that, can't you, folks? It's the practical way of doing things." Expert deceit.

Q. Is there a controlled anger in the way you characterize the legislature?

A. Yes, I believe there's a controlled anger here! "Legislatures," however, does *not* refer to Washington men or Springfield men! (Perhaps you would have liked it better if I'd said "legislatings.")

Q. I'm trying to press the point that your poetry in its most recent form is more socially aware than in the earlier work.

A. Yes, although many people hated *The Bean Eaters*; such people as would accuse me of forsaking lyricism for polemics, despised *The Bean Eaters* because they said that it was "getting too social. Watch it, Miss Brooks!" [Laughs] They didn't like "The Lovers of the Poor"; they didn't like "The

Chicago Defender Sends a Man to Little Rock: Fall, 1957," which I don't care too much about—or at least I'd like to remove that last line ["The loveliest lynchee was our Lord"].

Q. How do you feel about some of your other poems, now that you've mentioned those with specific social commentary? Is it fair to classify them in the same way—for example, the "Beverley Hills, Chicago" poem or "A Bronzeville Mother Loiters in Mississippi. Meanwhile, a Mississippi Mother Burns Bacon"?

A. I couldn't put these poems in a second little book, under the title "Social Poems," "Social Speech." I just feel that they're poems. I think that the wonderment or resentment is inside the person who is making the accusation, if it is an accusation, and usually when people talk about the social content of the poems, they are accusing you of doing something dastardly.

Q. I didn't mean to do that. But one more point. You wrote in 1950 that poetry must do double duty: "At the present time, poets who happen also to be Negroes are twice-tried. They have to write poetry, and they have to remember that they are Negroes." Then several lines later: "They are likely to find significances in those subjects not instantly obvious to their fairer fellows. The raindrop may seem to them to represent racial tears. . . . The golden sun might remind them that they are burning.[3]

A. That's carrying it a stretch too far, as poets will do, I suppose; but at least in Chicago we have had spirited conversations about whether a black poet has the right to deal with trees, to concern himself with trees. And one of the things that I've always said was, certainly, certainly a black poet may be involved in a concern for trees, if only because when he looks at one he thinks of how his ancestors have been lynched thereon. Well, that's a way of saying that in the black experience *everything* is important just as it is in the white experience.

Q. And it can be important in its own right, can't it? It is, of course, possible for anyone to look at a tree and see just a tree, or . . . ?

A. It is possible, but if a black person looks long enough, he just might think of other things that a white person might not . . . especially if you've seen some of the pictures in *Jet* magazine of what has happened on some of those trees—horrific.

---

[3] Langston Hughes, ed., *New Negro Poets U.S.A.* (Bloomington, Ind., 1964), p. 13.

Q. This comes around to what we were talking about at the beginning, that the black writer has more to see because perhaps more has happened to him.

A. That's probably true. He has the American experience and he also has the black experience; so he's very rich.

"My People Are Black People"

Ida Lewis / 1971

From *Essence Magazine* (April 1971), 26–31. Reprinted by permission of the Estate of Gwendolyn Brooks.

Lewis: How did you, a Pulitzer Prize winner, get turned on to the black revolution?

Brooks: The real turning point came in 1967, when I went to the Second Black Writers' Conference at Fisk University. I had been on tour and I was tired and wanted to get home, and I just thought I would whiz through Fisk, give my little reading, and come on back here to Chicago. But there I found what has stimulated my life these last three years: young people, full of a new spirit. They seemed stronger and taller, really ready to take on the challenges. Margaret Danner was there, another poet of my years, and she and I were both amazed to see what was happening. I was still saying "Negro," for instance. LeRoi Jones, who wasn't known yet as Imamu Amiri Baraka, arrived during our double offering. He came in while I was giving my reading, and I said, "Ah, there's LeRoi Jones," and everybody just went mad. The audience wasn't quite aware yet that he was the new messiah, but he was very much admired. We walked around all that day, looking at these new tokens and feeling so excited.

Later on, in the evening, LeRoi and Ron Milner gave a reading at Jubilee Hall. I was sitting beside a youngish white fellow. He had been very quiet. But when Baraka said at one point, "Up against the wall!" this man jumped to his feet and said, "Yeah, yeah, kill 'em!" And here he was, ordering his own execution. That's how electrified the atmosphere was. "Kill 'em all!" he said.

Lewis: So the conference was a kind of catalyst for you.

Brooks: Yes, but it wasn't the only thing. When I got home, I found a telegram from Oscar Brown, Jr., inviting em to a preview of his *Opportunity Please Knock,* a show he had developed out of the talents of the Blackstone Rangers. My daughter and a friend of hers excitedly went to the preview with me. And that was another stunner—to see what could be done if an older person took the time and had the interest to work with those youngsters.

The Blackstone Rangers are a teenage gang in Chicago of immense size and not all of the things they do are nice. I'm not sure just what to say about what they're doing now, because I'm not close to them. But I met some of them through Oscar Brown. I went up to him after the preview and said, "Oh, how wonderful that was!" It was, too. "Are there any writers among them?" I asked. "Because I would like to have a workshop for them if any of them are interested." I guess I'd been hearing about the Blackstone Rangers for a couple of years, and I'd had this yearning—it sounds funny, I know—to "do something for them."

Anyway, Oscar said that some of them did indeed want to write, and had in fact asked him if they could show me their manuscripts. He got in touch with Walter Bradford, a student at Wilson Junior College (now Kennedy-King College) in Chicago. Walter was a teenage organizer who had been working with some of these kids. He got about seven or eight of them together, and we started our class in the First Presbyterian Church, where they were rehearsing for their show. Every Friday I was downstairs teaching my group the intricacies of the sonnet form, and the cast was upstairs.

Lewis: What was the name of your group?

Brooks: It never had any name. We just got together and read our manuscripts and talked about them. These weren't the kind of young people you have a "workshop" for, so I stopped calling it even that. They used to laugh at me to beat the band for being interested in the sonnet and trying to teach them iambic pentameter. So finally, about six or eight months after we started, I quit and we just became friends. Then I gave Walter Bradford some material and some little guides and suggested that he organize a group of them. He did that and had a class of about twenty, and it was most successful.

In the meantime, some college students who had been coming to my group at the church kept on getting together, once a month here at my place. We only stopped last November because most of them are away now, some teaching, some working, others still in school. The house would open up, and all kinds of writers, dancers, painters, and just anybody young would come along in. It was a lot of fun, but we weren't getting any real writing done. The best thing to come out of our group, I think, is an anthology that Dudley Randall will bring out soon called *Jump Bad.*

Lewis: When did you get interested in writing?

Brooks: My mother says I began to write poetry—putting rhymes together, that is—when I was seven. I have notebooks dating from the time I was eleven, when I started to keep my poems in composition books. My mother decided that I was to be the female Paul Laurence Dunbar. I believed every word she said and just kept on writing. Sometimes I turned out two and three poems or a couple of stories in one day, all very, very, very bad.

Lewis: What were the themes of these poems?

Brooks: Nature, love, death, the sky. I was very much infatuated with the sky. I would sit on the back porch and look up there and see the clouds and pretend things, particularly about my future. I think my dreams were based on the fairy tales I was reading. The future was very vague, but it was very beautiful; it had a fascinating sort of glamour. So that's what those poems were made of.

Lewis: Were you a loner as a young girl?

Brooks: I had friends, but I felt alone inside. Maybe this is how every young girl feels. I was not the popular kind of little girl who takes to everybody. I always felt ill at ease, except with the children on my block. When I went to school, it was really like being in another world. I felt that all the kids were strangers, and I felt inferior to everybody.

Lewis: Why was that?

Brooks: All I can say is that I enjoyed writing, and those few who knew about it thought it was a ridiculous thing to be doing. They figured there must be something odd about me that I would want to stay in my room and write instead of going to dances. But in the neighborhood I felt sort of brassy, as though those were my friends, more or less. Still, my happiest times were when I was by myself, writing or reading. I read a great deal—sometimes a couple of books a day. I'd go to the library and get out poetry, or often some little juvenile novel. I read *Caroling Dusk,* which introduced me to a good many writers of our race I'd never heard of before. I read Langston Hughes's *Weary Blues,* for example, and got very excited about what he was doing. I realized that writing about the ordinary aspects of black life was important.

Lewis: Were your parents a great influence in your life?

Brooks: Yes. I had a wonderful father who really took time with his children. He read us stories and sang songs. When I think of him, I think of the word "kind." He was a janitor, though he had wanted to be a doctor, and he'd studied pre-med at Fisk for about a year and a half. But then he got married and had to take care of a family, so he didn't have any money and had to let his ambitions go. I remember his being a very rich sort of person.

He was always giving of himself. He talked about injustices, too; he told us often about the race riots that he had seen in 1919. He knew that things were not right. But he didn't allow that to make our home an unhappy one.

I remember home as being a place where little joys stuck out of a pretty steady base of—not contentment; what shall I call it?—maybe comfort and openness. We were at ease with each other in the house. We celebrated all the holidays. We made a great deal out of Christmas. Sometimes all of us would go look for the Christmas tree and come back with it together. Easter was a time to have pretty new clothes. This doesn't mean that we got rich off my father's pay as a janitor. We were very, very poor at times during the Depression, which I still remember sharply. When he made $25 a week, that was great. Sometimes the McKinley Music Company, where his job was, wouldn't have enough work, and he would come home with $10 or even $8. Then we would have beans.

My mother subscribed to duty. She believed that everyone should do what he or she was supposed to do, and she brought us up correctly. She made us eat properly, and encouraged us in anything of an intellectual nature. Mama had been a teacher before she got married. She was glad that I liked to read and that my brother drew.

Lewis: What are your memories of high school?

Brooks: A thing that I recall clearly, I guess because it has to do with my writing, was that there was a school paper and I wanted to get something printed in it. I think I sent in a couple of things, but they weren't published. Then came a day when I had to write a review of a novel called *Janice Meredith* by P. L. Ford. It was a required paper, and the mark on it was going to be a very important part of our final grade. But I hated the book, and I didn't even read all of it. So I decided to write my review in rhyme and put some humor in it, too. This way I could enlarge on my small amount of information and use my imagination. Sure enough, that was the "right" thing to do, because the teacher was very much impressed. You must remember that in those days not every Tom, Dick, Harry, Jane, or Josephine was writing poetry. Certainly very few children were. So she gave me an A on the paper and became very interested in me, and she said she thought that I had a future. Around the same time I joined the journalism class, and that teacher said the same thing.

No blacks were teaching in that school, which was Englewood High. I'd gone to several high schools previously. I'd spent one year at Hyde Park

Branch, which I hated. It was my first experience with many whites around. I wasn't much injured, just left alone. I realized that they were a society apart, and they really made you feel it. None of them would have anything to do with you, aside from some white boy if he "fell in love" with you.

Then I went to Wendell Phillips for a year, and I didn't like it either. The kids were what would now be called hip. The school was solid, solid black, and that's why I thought I would like it. The girl who lived next door to me on 43rd and Champlain had been telling me I'd "have a ball" there, so I transferred. But I felt really inferior because I was not one of the girls who danced and went to parties and played the kissing games. I wasn't up to that. I just slumped through the halls, quiet, hugging my books. I had about two friends, if that many. Then I left and went to Englewood, and graduated from it. Englewood was a mixed school; I seemed to get along better there, though I still wasn't popular. There, *all* blacks were somewhat Alone.

Lewis: Did you ever wish that you were popular?

Brooks: Oh, yes. But I wasn't willing even to try to become so. It seemed impossible to change myself entirely, and I was sure I would fail as "that kind" of girl. Furthermore, there was another problem, the color bar. It was very strong then, not that I'm going to say it's all over with now. A dark-complexioned girl just didn't have a chance if there was light-skinned competition. In grammar school I got my first introduction to the fact that bias could exist among our people, too. In my novel *Maud Martha,* I have a scene where a little boy wants to put a little light girl in his wagon but not a darker girl, and when she tries to be casual about everything, he says, oh, shut up, you old black gal. That kind of thing happened every other day.

At least now they have the phrase "Black is beautiful," and although a lot of people say we ought to stop using it because it's not adequate, I believe it can't be said too much.

Lewis: What did you do after high school?

Brooks: I went to Wilson Junior College. It got started just in the nick of time—the September after I graduated from high school. If it hadn't opened its doors right then, perhaps I would not have had those two years of college I did get.

Lewis: Did you have any direct contact with established writers then?

Brooks: Let's skip back to when I was sixteen. Not the kind of sweet sixteen that got all decked out in organza, I assure you. What made sixteen important for me was that I decided to write to James Weldon Johnson and ask him what he thought about some of my poems. He wrote back. I've still got that letter somewhere. I have two letters from him, in fact. In one, he told me that I was talented but that I needed to read modern poetry. This was a great help to me. I already knew the work of such people as Langston Hughes and Countee Cullen. Then I began to read others, T. S. Eliot, Ezra Pound, and e. e. cummings—never could stand cummings, though, until I heard him read his own poetry on a record.

I met Johnson in person as well, thanks to my mother. She had all kinds of "nerve," and when he came to our church to give a speech, she took me to hear him. We were both so excited because, after all, the great man had written to me. My mother told me to go up to him afterward.

James Weldon Johnson was very erect, handsome, and tall. When his speech was over, he stood there, coldly receiving the plaudits of those who had come, not smiling at all. I really didn't want to show him my things and was already beginning to feel two inches tall, but my mother insisted we go through with it. So we went up to him, and seeing I wasn't going to say anything, she said, "This is my daughter," and told him my name. Then she said, "She is the one who sent you those poems, and you wrote to her." And he replied, "I get so many of them, you know." And that was all he had to say. So we came away disgruntled, chastised, properly put in our places.

Not long after that Langston Hughes came to give a reading at the Metropolitan Community Church and he was altogether different. We went through the same rigmarole. I hadn't written to him, but my mother had brought a whole pack of my stuff, and we showed it to him. He read it right there; he said that I was talented and must go on writing. He was really an inspiration.

Lewis: Did you have any formal training outside of school?

Brooks: Yes. A poetry class for young blacks was starting at the Southside Community Art Center in Chicago and I joined. Inez Cunningham Stark opened this class. A fantastic woman. She was a reader for *Poetry* magazine and was very wealthy. She was a real rebel. She flew in the face of her society tradition, coming among blacks on the Southside. (People would tell her she'd be raped.) She gave us an education in modern poetry. I had been reading modern poetry, but I didn't know anything about technique, what writers of the day were doing and how they were doing it. She had us come over to her beautiful apartment on what Chicagoans call the Gold Coast, and many of us saw that kind of life for the first time. It was several kinds of eyeopeners to me. This class of hers was very alive. We were encouraged to tear each other to pieces. We would try to say *exactly* what we thought about each other's writings, something I haven't seen in any classes in this time of ours.

Lewis: Is that good?

Brooks: It helped me to have somebody tell me what he thought was wrong with my work, and then to bounce the analysis back and forth. Some people went home crying, But they usually came back. I remember Mrs. Stark sponsored a little poetry contest for us, and I won first place. One of the judges was S. I. Hayakawa. S. I. Hayakawa was a great liberal in those days. The way he's narrowed is a lesson I hope that I'll be able to keep seeing "the light," and marching in accordance with it. You can't stop growing— I'm growing now. I have certainly changed from where I was back in only 1967. I knew there were injustices, and I wrote about them, but I didn't know what was behind them. I didn't know what kind of society we live in. I didn't know it was all organized.

Lewis: During the 1940s and 1950s, how did you view the black world?

Brooks: I thought that integration was the solution. All we had to do was keep on appealing to the whites to help us, and they would.

Lewis: Why did you think that?

Brooks: Because I relied heavily on Christianity. People were really good, I thought; there was some good even in people who seemed to be evil. It's true that I didn't know very much about wicked people or who they were. It was a good world, the best of all possible worlds. I believed everything. But then I wasn't reading the books I should have read, when I was young. If I'd been reading W. E. B. DuBois, I would have known more, but I didn't even hear of *The Souls of Black Folk* until I was well grown.

I read chiefly for entertainment in those days. Perhaps the deepest thing I read was Ralph Waldo Emerson's *Self-Reliance* (and *Compensation:* if you lost something here, you got it in some form over there. That thought made me happy.)

Lewis: Not a very worldly-wise view.

Brooks: Oh, not at all. I didn't know anything. I was naive, I was shy, and a very sweet girl. Sweet and ignorant. Some of it stuck—until 1967. What I saw and heard at the Fisk Black Writers' Conference was of a new nature to me. Later, the kids in my writing class would talk about what was going on.

And I'd listen and say, "What? You don't mean it! Is that really true?" A case in point was The Wall. That was something new, to see all those black people out on the street together, loving each other. Phil Cohran's group, the Artistic Heritage Ensemble, played music; the poets read—I read. It was wonderful.

Lewis: Can you pinpoint the differences in perspective?

Brooks: The most striking difference was that they just didn't countenance integration. That was out. I had been asleep. If I had been reading even the newspaper intelligently, I too would have seen that it simply was not working, that there was too much against it, that blacks kept exposing themselves to it only to get their faces smacked. (At the least.) The thing to stress was black solidarity and pride in one's brothers and sisters. People didn't instruct me. They didn't sit me down and say, "Now, we're going to give you your lesson for today." I just picked it up by osmosis, listening to them and watching what they did. I went around with them sometimes and heard them giving readings. Listening to them was wonderful. They speak out of themselves so well. These are true poets.

Lewis: Who was the audience for black poets before? Who supported your readings, for example?

Brooks: Chiefly whites, of course.

Lewis: Did you feel comfortable with that situation?

Brooks: At the time, I hadn't really broken the question down like that. Blacks didn't seem to be buying our people's work in great quantity, not even Langston Hughes's books. It was whites who were reading and listening to us, salving their consciences—our accusations didn't hurt too much. But I was repeatedly called bitter. White people would come up after a reading and say, "Why are you so bitter? Don't you think things are improving?"

That's the glorious thing about today: we aren't con-concerned about what whites think of our work. In one of Horace Bond's African rhetoric classes at Kansas University, one man, a young teacher there, asked me, "What have you got to say about these critics who tell us we're not writing universally and we don't know how to put our words together?

I said, "What do you care? We don't care about these notions anymore. Whites are not going to understand what is happening in black literature today. Even those who want to sympathize with it still are not equipped to be proper critics." I told him that we are developing our own critics—Stanley Crouch, Addison Gayle, Clayton Riley, Larry Neal, Ezekiel Mphahlele.

By then I had opened my eyes. And I think I've had some hand since in spreading this new spirit. I saw how proud and how strong blacks were becoming. Their confidence in themselves was inspiring. They knew they were right; they had the essentials. Our people are kind of rattled now. They don't have so much certainty as in those good years of 1967 and 1968, though I'm sure this is just an aspect of the growing that has to be done.

Lewis: How has this new awareness changed your life?

Brooks: In the 1950s and early 1960s, I was still a loner, I had a few black friends and a few white friends. I would go to their homes, they would come to my home, and that was about the extent of my meaningful social relationships. I used to give great big literary parties, too, cramping more than a hundred people into this house. I did the same when we lived in a little apartment on East 63rd Street, (where I had a great party for Langston Hughes.) I thought I was happy, and I saw myself going on like that the rest of my days. I thought it was the way to live. I wrote, these people wrote, we saw each other, we talked about writing. But it was white writing, the different trends among whites. Today I am conscious of the fact that—my people are black people; it is to them that I appeal for understanding.

Lewis: How did these whites regard you?

Brooks: They thought I was lovely. I was a sort of pet. They thought I was nice, and I was nice. I believed in integration, and so did they. Almost anytime they'd have a gathering, I'd be one of them. But now, I rarely see these people, though a couple still call themselves my friends.

Lewis: Do you miss those you don't associate with any more?

Brooks: No. But you see, I couldn't. That would be impossible. I just don't think "that way" anymore.

Lewis: How has it been to be a poet and a family woman?

Brooks: My husband and I were both writing when we got married. But I'd always felt that it was the marriage that should get most of a wife's attention. So I wrote when other things did not call upon me. I do know that there was about a year—after the birth of my first child—when I scarcely put pen to paper; but except for that, I managed to keep at it. I gave a lot of attention to my children. I do not regret doing that.

My husband and I are separated now. We got along very well on the plain levels of companionship. We could talk to each other about anything—writing, politics. He put up with a great deal. Of course I wasn't traveling so much during our marriage as I am now, but he encouraged me in my writing all along. He was very pleased when any good thing happened to me, though I know that, being a man, he did have problems adjusting to what I was doing. Often we discussed his own literary ambitions. He hasn't really put them to test yet. He has sent stories out occasionally, but not many. He's an excellent writer, incidentally, and he should have gotten a book out years ago. When he does, I'm sure that it will get a great deal of attention.

When I began to subscribe so enthusiastically and almost without question to the new, young movements among blacks, he didn't agree because he was and still is an integrationist. But this had nothing to do with our breakup. Nor was it caused by "other women" or "other men." I can at least say *this:* I don't believe in breaking up a marriage on such grounds. I believe that if there is any substance to a marriage, an infidelity should not bring about a divorce.

Lewis: That's an old-fashioned view, you know.

Brooks: There were different reasons for the outlook in past years. The woman, for one thing, was far more dependent economically than she is today. Often she couldn't get a job, or would have a very hard time taking care of her children if she did. This is less true today.

I can say that I have no intention of ever getting married again. No, not to God. One general reason for this decision is that marriage is a hard, demanding state. Especially if you're a woman, you have to set yourself aside constantly. Although I did it during my marriage, I couldn't again. After having had a year of solitude, I realize that this is what is right for me, to be able to control my life.

Brooks: That really sounds like the old flapper days. Well, I have been doing exactly what I wanted to do. I mentioned before that I've been sponsoring writing contests. For example, I started one at the Burnside Elementary School here. The school had given a program in my honor, and in my thank-you speech, I suddenly found myself saying, "I'm going to sponsor a poetry contest here. Would you kids like to have a poetry contest? "Yeah!" "I'll give you $100 for four prizes, and your teachers can be the judges. You'll have time to write your poems, and then you'll get the prizes." I went on to high schools and then to colleges like Fisk University and Indiana University. And I started offering an annual Poet Laureate Award last spring—that's $500 for the two best high school poets.

Lewis: So you give all your money away?

Brooks: That's what I've been doing. And while money as such isn't all that important, earning and controlling it is symbolic of independence—for me, for all women.

Lewis: Does the black woman have a special responsibility to be independent, to redefine her role in life?

Brooks: I feel that she does, and that it's not an easy job in these strange days. The men are forging "forward" now, too. They have a new belief in themselves, and one of the things many of them are determined not to be loaded with is conventional attachments to women—like marriage.

Relations between men and women seem disordered to me. I was asked recently how I felt about Women's Lib. I think Women's Lib is not for black women for the time being, because black men *need* their women beside them, supporting them in these very tempestuous days. I made this comment in Horace Bond's class as well, and a young man asked me, "What do you mean, 'for the time being'?"

I said, "Well, that will depend on how you men treat us. As our struggle goes on, if you treat us considerately, we may never need to subscribe to "the movement." But if you don't, who knows what we'll have to do in the future?" I did say that it's entirely wrong, of course, for women to be denied the same job income men have. When it comes to that, black women should be fighting for equal pay just as white women should.

Lewis: But the young black girl today does not seem to be naturally attracted to Women's Lib. What should she do as an alternative?

Brooks: She should find the men who don't force her to stand separate. Isn't that the new decision, that men and women are to work together in this revolution?

Lewis: Do you think young women today want to get married?

Brooks: Yes, they still want to get married. All those I know look forward to marriage with the Right Man.

Lewis: But you are down on marriage for yourself?

Brooks: I'm not young. I'm 53. My children are grown. I'm not saying I'm down on marriage; it just will not fit in with my life. I like to be alone more than a married woman can be. I love being in this house by myself. I want to be able to give my attention to writing, reading, and doing whatever else occurs to me rather than fixing three meals a day and humoring a man. My husband, I believe, would give me credit for *this:* he knew that I always upheld his faith in himself. I wouldn't talk about my own affairs unless he brought them up, and I tried to make sure that things I said would not be taken amiss.

I know a lot of women feel they're always walking on eggs. In my case, part of it was due to the fact that we both wrote. It's hard on the man's ego to be married to a woman who happens to get some attention before he does. But I must give my husband this—of all men in that position, I believe he behaved better than anybody I could imagine. He really did have a great interest in my succeeding. He was a very good critic, too. He used to criticize my work. "Criticize" sounds a little harsh; he would read my work and tell me how he thought I could improve it.

Lewis: Did you take his advice often?
Brooks: Oh, yes.

Lewis: What are you writing now?
Brooks: I'm bringing my autobiography to an end, and I expect Broadside Press to publish it. This, by the way, is another big change in my life. I've been telling everybody who's black, "You ought to have a black publisher," and of course that was easy for me to say. I've been with Harper's since 1945, when it published my first book, and I had meant for it to bring out my autobiography.

Lewis: The autobiography must represent quite a shift of focus for a poet. Have you planned other innovations?
Brooks: You know, I've just recently begun to realize that all kinds of things could be possible for me if I only had the nerve—for instance, other forms of writing that I had not considered myself capable of doing or really interested in doing, because I had imagined myself writing nothing else but poetry the rest of my life.

One project I've been mulling over is an annual. I would like, when I get some money, to bring out a little book once a year that would be composed only of essays or position papers written by knowledgeable blacks. Something else that's very much on my mind is fiction. I'm planning a series of short novels now. How exactly I'm going to write them I'm not sure. That's a whole new, exciting department in itself. But I *have* decided to keep them to only about 15,000 or 25,000 words each, and do you know why? I want them to be read by people who generally don't have a long attention span. It's not a question of "writing down" to them. It's that they are simply not interested in going through a book running 600,000 words. My idea is that we have got to reach the audience the poets are reaching by going to taverns. I've been with them, and I've seen how that happens—how the drinking comes to a stop so that people can hear the words, words which are relevant to *them.*

Lewis: You really seem as though you're starting a new life spiritually.

Brooks: It's true that my life is developing new dimensions. A concrete example, that serves pretty well metaphorically, is that I got on an airplane for the first time last spring. That really opened up geography to me. Now I just run up the "gangplank." This is what the last three years have been like for me: a challenge, bringing more freedom of movement. It's just fine to be airborne.

Interview with Gwendolyn Brooks

Hoyt Fuller, Eugenia Collier, George Kent,
Dudley Randall / 1973

From *In the Memory and Spirit of Frances, Zora, and Lorraine: Essays and Interviews on Black Women and Writing* edited by Juliette Bowles (Washington, D.C.: Institute for the Arts and the Humanities/Howard University, 1979). Reprinted with permission of the Moorland-Spingarn Research Center, Howard University.

Hoyt Fuller: Does a poem ever come more or less in the form in which you eventually have it published? Does it come through to you complete?

Gwendolyn Brooks: A poem rarely comes whole and completely dressed. As a rule, it comes in bits and pieces. You get an impression of something—you feel something, you anticipate something, and you begin, feebly, to put these impressions and feelings and anticipation or rememberings into those things which seem so common and handleable—words.

And you flail and you falter and you shift and you shake, and finally, you come forth with the first draft. Then, if you're myself and if you're like many of the other poets that I know, you revise, and you revise. And often the finished product is nothing like your first draft. Sometimes it is.

Fuller: How much time do you spend from the conception of the idea for the poem to the actual creation of the poem, and in the shape that you want to have it published?

Brooks: Sometimes 15 minutes; sometimes 15 months. There is no recipe for writing a poem, I believe, or for getting through with it in a certain amount of time. That's not important. The job has its own special requirements, and that's it.

George Kent: Is there any poem which you think very well of indeed which you have written and which came in a very short period of time?

Brooks: "Think very well of"? "The Old Marrieds," an average poem, which I tolerate, didn't take long to write. It's very simple, not that I mean to say that a simple poem takes a small amount of time. The very simple-looking poem, "We Real Cool", was written over a period of years. Well, I mean it was finished over a period of years, by going back to it from time to

67

time, changing this and changing that. But "The Old Marrieds" at least required no special agony.

Randall: Yesterday you said you don't yet have any poems about your journey to Africa but you are going to write some and you have notes. That made me wonder whether you wrote with "emotion recollected in tranquility"? Is that the way you write?

Brooks: No. I do make a lot of notes. I make notes on the scene at the moment of 'inspiration'—and I'm really not afraid of that word. But "emotion recollected in tranquility"? It seems to me that there has to be some kind of agitation within you in order to produce any kind of poem. So while I'm writing, I'm agitated, and I like to be. I like to start very close to the time that I've taken the notes. This isn't always possible but that's my preference.

Randall: Do you find that with some subjects, an idea for a poem might incubate a great deal longer than other subjects? For instance, if you have not yet produced poems which grow out of your African experience, it may be that the poems are still incubating.

Brooks: I guess "incubating" is a rather disturbing word, isn't it? To use in this way but I imagine that's just about right.

Now, in part of my autobiography, I have a little section called "African Fragments." And there are bits and pieces there of impressions that I had while I was in Africa, which I expect to extend. But they have not come to flower. That would be a case of "emotion recollected in tranquility"—well, no, no—I still want to exclude the word, "tranquility."

Collier: You pinpoint a change in your poetry to November 1967 when you perhaps became more aware of the current black ideology and expression. What we have been talking about is a change of themes. Has there been a corresponding change in form? You're not writing sonnets any more.

Brooks: No, I'm not writing sonnets, and I probably won't be, because, as I've said many times, this does not seem to me to be a sonnet time. It seems to be a free verse time, because this is a raw, ragged, uneven time—with rhymes, if there are rhymes, incidental and random.

I am in transition. I want to reach all manner of black people. That's my urgent compulsion, to write a kind of poetry that will not be an imitation of younger blacks, although I admire their work so much, but will be a—some special kind of Gwendolynian poem that will not have the close-textured quality of some of the sonnets I've written, perhaps, or a poem like "A Light and Diplomatic Bird" which I used to like so much because of its embroideries, or certain parts of *The Anniad*. It will be a simple-looking poem but there will be subtleties easily reached, I hope, by those who are interested in reaching them—immediately enjoyable by black people who spend a great deal of their time in taverns or the streets, blacks who, perhaps, have dropped out of high school. I still want to reach and appeal to such blacks.

Randall: What do you do about complexity versus simplicity? Have you tried to make your poem available to, say, men in bars or on street corners? What are you going to do about this complexity which you already have? Do you think you'll lose it?

Brooks: Well, that'll be all right. If that's to be, that's to be. I like George's [Kent] saying yesterday that "In The Mecca" is a transitional poem. That was in transition from a state of—well, a state of semi-smugness to the first department of liberation. And now, I'm in a second transitional stage that will result, I hope, in some form or forms that will do the things I've just outlined must be done.

Kent: Do you feel that there is any necessary conflict between complexity of theme and simplicity of presentation?

Brooks: I don't think that my final solution to this problem will exclude reflection, beautiful imagery, music, "lyricism"—that word is almost a cliche now—and approaches the problems that are aroused at the sound of the word, "universality." Shortness, for me, is part of the solution. Take a poem like "The Rhyme of the Ancient Mariner." You may remember it as a simple poem, but there are many complexities in that language.

Randall: Gwen, after you appeared at my class at the University of Detroit, students wrote short papers on their reactions to you. One student said you used a lot of words that the average person wouldn't understand. And he listed the words. For instance, in "The Kitchenette Building," you used the word, "aria" and at the beginning of "In the Mecca," you have "Mies Van der Rohe." Do you contemplate changing your diction or your vocabulary?

Brooks: Of course I intend to change such things as that, Dudley. And I know that you know this. That is the whole problem—that I realize, that I recognize.

Randall: But I explained to him, I said, "She has a wonderful vocabulary, a large vocabulary. She wants to be precise, so she uses the precise word."

Brooks: Well, I'll have to find some other words. And yet I can hardly change the architect's name from Mies Van der Rohe to, say, Missy. I've gone in Chicago to taverns with some of these young poets, where we read our work. And the people there will respond to a poem like "We Real Cool." They don't have any trouble with that.

But if I read parts of "In The Mecca", or even such a poem as "Kitchenette Building," they would empathize with such, I'm sure. But you can't count on their taking the time for careful listening. In a tavern, the people are busy or drunk or sick. And they're are not going to spend all that time with you, so you have got to find some way of engaging them imediately, and if possible, bloodboilingly. So, I'm perfectly willing to leave out the word, "aria."

Kent: If I can complicate this a little bit more—there's a blues lyric which in part goes, "I got a gal way 'cross town, she crochet all the time / I got a gal way 'cross town, she crochet all the time / Baby, if you don't stop crocheting, you're gonna lose your mind." Now, what does crochet mean in that poem? How many people feel they know what crochet means in that poem?

Brooks: Oh, don't you think more black people know about crocheting? It has to do with needles and thread and—my grandmother, she crocheted.

Kent: I said—pardon me, I said, what does it mean in the poem?

Randall: Well, George, suppose you tell us? (Laughter)
Brooks: Maybe I'm missing something.

Kent: What I'm trying to get at—I'm sure I'm not successful, because Blind Lemon Jefferson probably communicates some of this by tone, and also by context. But it means sexual intercourse.
Brooks: I didn't know that. (Laughter)

Kent: What I'm getting at is, it seems to me that the simplicity is the very difficult thing to define. Ordinarily, I think people look at blues lyrics as representing a very good level of simplicity, where there are certain conventions of metaphor in blues lyrics, which if you haven't familiarized yourself with to some degree, may be confusing, especially if you're no longer in that immediate country blues community.

(From Audience:) I would like for you to comment on all the very beautiful things that you've done with black women in your poetry.
Brooks: I don't know whether all the women in the poetry are very beautiful or not. Did you think—well, I no longer believe there is one ideal black

woman. I think that there are different kinds of black women who are all doing effective things.

It isn't absolutely necessary that your ideal black woman have three or four children. A woman who has no children can be doing something very important for her race. Now, this is a different idea from what we thought just a few years ago. We seemed to feel that a woman must have children, must get married.

It's important to remember, though, that the children are here and are going to be the citizens, our black citizens of tomorrow. So whatever we can do to help children is important. And it can be a very immediate and seemingly small thing. This summer, I myself have decided to corral the children in my block*—there are about 30 of them—into a sort of summer reading and writing club. And I'll have them come over once a week and I'll introduce them to the books that I think are helpful, as well as interesting, and we'll talk about them and I'll ask them to express their feelings in little poems and stories and essays. And I think that might be helpful in a small way. If it works, others may want to do the same thing.

(From Audience:) What is the meaning of the title of the autobiography? (*Report from Part One*)

Brooks: It merely means a report from the first part of my life. A report. Somebody says I'm going to write another one. I didn't know that. That one was horrifyingly agonizing, and I don't have a good memory. I know I left out a lot that I wanted to include. There were some things that I meant to leave out, of course.

(From Audience:) At one point in your autobiography, you wrote that it frightened you to realize that "If I had died before the age of 50, I'd have died a Negro fraction." How seriously is that to be taken?

Brooks: That's to be taken utterly seriously. Before I was 50, I hadn't met these young people such as Don Lee, especially, who, without sitting me down and telling me—I mean, they're always giving me all this honor, and saying how honorable I am, et cetera—but if it hadn't been for them, I wouldn't know what I do now about our time, our condition. And I don't know everything yet about our society. And I feel it's absolutely necessary

---

*(Didn't "corral" the 30, instead started a forum for the 18 highschoolers on the block. I kept it going four years.

G. Brooks, August 1979)

for you to know something about the society you live in. These people, as I say, didn't sit me down and give me my lessons but they were kind enough to feel that I was interested in knowing something more than I knew. They allowed me to associate with them, and by a sort of osmosis I learned a lot that I never dreamed of. My eyebrows were always going up with each new knowledge.

(From Audience:) Are you saying that you learned something about their point of view, or—what exactly?

Brooks: I mean they helped—well, first of all, they helped me to see what is happening here. They also—

(From Audience:) You didn't see it before then?

Brooks: No. I know that sounds incredible but my stupidity, my ignorance, were incredible. I hadn't read. That is one concrete thing that they did for me—they introduced me to reading I should know, that all of us should know. I hadn't even read *The Autobiography of Malcolm X* before I met them. I hope that puts to rest those rumors that I was an inspiration to these people, which is always being said here and there, and it's not so.

(A brief, and not entirely audible, exchange takes place at this point between persons in audience and panel and ends with a participant commenting, "We shall overcome.")

Brooks: Yes, yes, we must overcome. In that connection, I think I'll take out a little time to read you some notes that I meant to read to you on another occasion—but quite in line with what you're asking there, quite in line with it. I said, "Some of the young people who taught me to be strong have disappeared from the field of the fever. They no longer love their own. They no longer announce that black is beautiful. They keep adding, so is white, as if there weren't enough mouths in the world assuring us of that."

"But I really believed what they told me in 1967. I still believe it. I shall not veer with the veerers." Then I say dramatically, "Come back, black people, come on back. Recognize the divisionary tactic. Do not subscribe to 'Superfly, *irresponsible* abortion"—and I shall read my abortion poem later on, on another occasion—"money worship, sly brain soiling"—and I think we may not be using that word "brainwashing" right—"brain soiling attempts to make you think little of your people, to make you'—in big letters here—"THINK WHITE."

"Be on your guard against the sly brainsoilers, the division tacticians, even if they are our parents, even if they are spouses, even if they are children, lovers, brothers, sisters, uncles, aunts, treasured neighbors, white friends, black friends, employers, teachers, respected writers, elected representatives in court and castle.

"Keep your eyes open, your minds aware. Do not be ashamed of ignorance. Be ashamed only of an unwillingness to find out. As for the veerers, we realize that to err is human. Come back. We welcome you back with open arms." That's it.

(From Audience:) What can we do to counterbalance the influence of the veerers?

Brooks: Well, this-you'll probably hate me for saying—but this is one of the advantages of age. When you have lived to be 55, as I have, you realize that things come and things go. And that which is not usable is really sifted out by time. And in this case, I don't think it's going to be necessarily a *lot* of time. I don't know what else we can do except to express our views. Many of us have as much attention as those who are spreading an unfortunate story.

(A question is raised from audience which is not entirely audible on tape. The question referred to a job Miss Brooks held with a spiritual advisor in the old Mecca building.)

Brooks: I was there only four months and then I was fired because I wouldn't become his assistant pastor in the little church he had next door. That was, as I remember it, the most miserable part of my life. I felt soiled in that employ. It was my very first job, typing. And I didn't feel right in that situation. But is there any other influence that you think it might have had on me that I'm not picking up from you? How am I spiritually? That's a very intelligent question. And I can give only a sprawling sort of answer. I go to a church with my mother on Mother's Day and, as a rule, on Easter. I haven't sorted out all my feelings about religion yet. There are many things that I don't understand.

I don't understand, for instance, why babies have to suffer the things they do in this world of ours, and yet many of a religious inclination tell me that all this will be explained on the other side and that all I have to do is just wait. That dose not seem to be sensible.

And other parts of that question I need to do more pondering on. However— well, I'm not flying anymore, as you know because my train was two hours late today. But until I stopped flying in December, I got on planes and loved the experience but found myself saying, always, as soon as I sat down, please God, protect us all. Now, perhaps you people can tell me what that means.

Black Books Bulletin Interviews
Gwen Brooks
Haki Madhubuti / 1974

From *Black Books Bulletin* 2 (1974), 25–28. Copyright 1974, reprinted by permission of Third World Press, Inc., Chicago, Illinois.

BBB: Gwen, we would like to start off by asking you a question that has probably been asked of you quite a bit, but we believe that it is fundamental in our understanding of you and your work. Why do you write?

Brooks: That question has been asked many times before and I've sort of divided my writing life into three parts. I wrote in the first department which started at the age of seven, or so my mother tells me, and ends about the age of thirteen, to "express myself." I wrote about dandelions and clouds, love and enemies, friends, anything that seemed sort of nice around me and my environs. This department ended about when I was thirteen when I went to Hyde Park high school here in Chicago, which was then chiefly white, and that was my first study exposure to prejudice because of race. I then wrote a poem, a sonnet which I named "To the Hinderer," and this was the beginning of my integration stage. I began to sense that if we screamed loudly enough and showed how truly wonderful we were, that sooner or later they would open up their arms and embrace us and invite us to share the feast. I kept believing that until 1957. This was the third department of my writing activity. And then because of the new young influences, Don L. Lee chiefly among them, I began to understand that Black Afrikans should be concerned about Blackness. And I believe with Don and other young writers that Black poetry is written by Blacks, about Blacks, to Blacks. That is where I am now and expect to stay.

BBB: Do you see anything in the present situation of Afrikans here in this country and on the continent that would cause you to think that we are likely to endure the future?

Brooks: That we are likely to endure the future?

BBB: That is in terms of Black people surviving. It seems that the greatest killer in the Black community is education and drugs. And of course the crime rates are very high. And we understand the reasons for this, but what strengths do you see within the context of our community which will allow us to survive the last quarter of the century?

Brooks: What strengths do I see within the community? I wouldn't want to be that specific, but I feel that Blacks are very strong, I look at what we have survived already. And I think that we ourselves, collectively, will develop answers for these threats, these oppressions. Perhaps we will have to be a little harder on ourselves than we have been. Perhaps from somewhere there will have to come a force that will really have to deal unmercifully with those elements.

BBB: Would you like to say a little bit about the workshop that you ran in the late sixties and early seventies? Especially the ones that you conducted with the Blackstone Rangers?

Brooks: I had only one workshop which as soon as the older people joined it was no longer called a workshop. I started it because I was excited by Oscar Brown Jr.'s show *Opportunity Please Knock*, and I asked him if there were some writers among those people, and if so, I would like to start a workshop for them. And a few of them came. That was a very interesting experience. They looked at me, I looked at them. I remember one who has kept up with me pretty much until the present; Peanuts, Richard Washington. He had a real interest in some of the younger Rangers and tried to be a good influence among them. But when the older people came, college students and community organizers, well, we became just a bunch of friends. We left the first Presbyterian Church and started meeting at my house where we are sitting now, this very day. And we had some very exciting times. They made it very plain that they did not want me to "teach" them anything about the sonnet form or such. Some of them feel a little different now and I don't know whether I should be happy about that or not. But, as I say, we were friends that talked about our poetry and read our poetry to each other. And also talked about what was going on in society. They taught me many things that I had not known before.

BBB: In keeping with that, what are some of the major changes in your life that have taken place over the last decade?

Brooks: Over the last decade, yes. Well, this is 1974. Well, my real changes came in 1967 when I first met those young people who could really see what was happening all around them and were kind enough to let me know too. They recommended books to me, that I read. Such books as *Report from Iron Mountain*, of the possibility and the desirability of peace, and *The*

Rich and the Super Rich and *The Choice*, which are books that I am always recommending to people now. Also the *Autobiography of Malcolm X* really influenced my changes.

BBB: One of the significant acts that we have noticed with you has been the consistent helping of Black institutions. We know that you are on the Board of Directors of the Institute of Positive Education and that you left Harper and Row for a Black publishing company in Detroit, Broadside Press. Would you comment on that?

Brooks: Yes. I didn't leave Harper and Row because they were doing anything to me. Or I didn't know of anything that they were doing to me that was of an evil nature. But I had been telling young poets to support the Black presses. Wherever I went to colleges to visit or to read my poetry, I would tell them that this was something that they should feel as a commitment. And it seemed strange for myself to continue with a white publishing company when I was giving this advice.

BBB: How have you found it working with Broadside Press? I know that one of the problems you had with Harper and Row was that your books were not widely distributed in the Black community. And we found also that in many cases they were not distributed outside of the continental U.S.A. In terms of production, do you see any qualitative difference between Harper and Row and Broadside Press?

Brooks: Well, about distribution, who would know better than BBB. Of course Black publishers have an immense problem with distribution. I think that we will have to continue to work with it, but there doesn't seem to me to be the great, great worry that some of us have felt it to be. I think that what a lot of young people told me in the late sixties was true. They believed that we should stress brotherhood and a caring for each other. And I think that Black writers, for the time being at least, will have to give up the idea of becoming millionaires, and famous and profiting at any level. They may even have to let go of a few dollars that they have to aid these presses so that they can attract future writers.

BBB: So essentially you are saying that Black writers should aid institutions, especially publishing institutions, and that they cannot hopefully, at this time, live off the returns that a book has made.

Brooks: Indeed no! You are asking me how I have found working with Broadside Press and I can include Third World Press there too. It's been an ideal experience. It really has been a working together.

BBB: In reading *Report from Part One*, the first part of your autobiography, it seems that you constantly revealed that an important part of your life involved conflict between you, the writer, and the individual family member. Maybe conflict is the wrong term, but you found that preserving the sacredness of your family is very important. How do you resolve the conflict between the artist and the family, if there is one? Are those three separate entities or are they one?

Brooks: We are talking about the family in the private sense, or the family in the extended sense?

BBB: We are talking about the family in the private sense.

Brooks: Well, with many Blacks there are going to be problems, but I think that that is just part of our growth. And those of us who are committed to Blackness and to the future and the nourishment of Blackness will have to strive straight ahead in spite of problems here and there along the way. But we are all living in interesting and dangerous times and we can expect problems, problems that are sometimes painful; sometimes deadly. The family, actually, is a major source of strength.

BBB: How do you propose to deal with the problems? For in many cases we talk about the "writer" or the "artist" being torn apart inside because of the individual or personal family problems. What would you suggest for the young writers in terms of dealing with his or her personal problems?

Brooks: Write about them.

BBB: We know that your work has changed greatly. When I say greatly we are talking about in terms of style. In the sense that there seems to be more of the quicker, sharper poems. It seems that these shorter and quicker poems communicate more effectively than the longer works. Also, we would like to know if you could possibly say now your work would have developed differently if you had read something like Chancellor Williams' *The Destruction of Black Civilization* as a young girl?

Brooks: I wish I might have had such an opportunity as a young girl, as a young woman, even ten years ago. But about changes in my style, I have not yet achieved the changes that I want. I was fascinated about seven years ago, when we used to go out, Don and me and the others, to taverns and other places and read our poetry. And I've always felt that it was most important that these people who make taverns their home still were able to find Don's poetry relevant and to sit there among the drinks and enjoy it and learn from it. If I had written [read] the intricate and embroidered sonnets, I'm sure that they would have thrown their drinks at me. And I want to develop a style that will appeal to these people, the people who make the streets their customary habitat, people in prisons. And of course I have to be very careful about including prisoners, because some of our best work is coming from prisons where people are at last having time to sit down and think over their lives and then to reflect, meditate and develop their thoughts in poetry and exciting fiction. This new style, I guess, should be rather short, because most people in this rushy time are not going to take time to sit down and read an epic. One exception to that might be a long poem such as Okot p'Biutek's "Song of Lawino," which is easy to get into and easy to stay into.

BBB: Speaking of writers, the Afrikan writer as an example, we found that out of the sixties, there was a wave of young writers producing, and in many cases functioning within the context of Black publishing houses. And we found that in some cases these writers were able to attract a following, but we find also that you had already established a following in the context of the Black and white literary world now leaving a major house and coming to a small Black publishing house and we found at the same time other "Black" writers leaving Black houses going to the white publishing houses. What do you think about that?

Brooks: I deplore it of course. I think that these people have decided that they want "success" in the American sense of the word. They want to turn out pretty little books. Although our own books are beautiful, they expect to make money, which is an illusion. I certainly never made money as a pub-lishee of Harper and Row and I began with them in 1945. I even published a novel there, *Maud Martha*, which I'm going to begin a brief sequel to this summer. Broadside Press will bring it out, but it's going to be very short. So, I'm very sorry that these people have wandered away and I hope that they will come back. Now I realize that Black publishers have some problems too. Some of these folks are saying that, well, we can't get published by Black publishers. I think that there is an answer to that and that is that we need more Black publishing companies. So instead of going to white companies I suggest that a few of them might get together and start yet another Black publishing company that is urgently needed.

BBB: You were in Africa a few years ago. Did your return home leave a mark on your future work: if so, how? And do you plan to return again soon?

Brooks: Ghana. I think only Ghana.

BBB: What are your plans for future work, novels, novella; you mentioned a small novel among others. What about biographical essays, what about political or literary essays? What are you working on now?

Brooks: I just finished a tiny book of poems called *Beckonings*. Some of the poems in there are an attempt at the new style we were talking about before. No essays. I plan to concentrate on poetry and fiction.

BBB: Are you your own worst critic?
Brooks: I think so.

BBB: In terms of your future work, do you plan on publishing any essays—collection of essays?
Brooks: I'm really not brilliant enough to bring out a book of essays.

BBB: What about literary reviews?
Brooks: I stopped writing reviews many years ago for that very reason. I think that people that write reviews should know about everything, should have read just about everything. And neither is true about myself.

BBB: You are now the editor of an annual publication called the *Black Position*. How has it been doing and what do you see as the future for it? What is coming out in the next issue?
Brooks: I don't think in terms of how it has been doing. I'm very happy about it. It has some excellent essays in it by the real Black thinkers of today, including Dudley Randall, Hoyt Fuller, Lerone Bennett, Don Lee, and this upcoming issue is going to feature a twenty-eight page interview with Chancellor Williams by George Kent. George Kent is interviewing him and has written an essay on the book, *Destruction of Black Civilization*. And it also features a long essay that I think is most provocative, and it's going to get letters, by Saundra Towns, and it's called "The Black Woman as Whore: The Genesis of the Myth." I think lots of people will write letters.

BBB: When is that issue coming out?
Brooks: In just a couple of weeks. We are waiting for page proofs. It also contains a chapter from Willie Kopsitsile's autobiography.

BBB: Who of the young writers today are moving and functioning as you see it in a correct direction?
Brooks: I'm sorry that you asked me that question because it's very difficult for me to say much on that score. Suffice it to say that if you are thinking about successors to Don L. Lee, these people who came up along at his time,

I can't name any. Among others, I like a lot of the work of Lucille Clifton. I think she is gathering more and more subscribers. I'm always meeting people who are asking if I've read her books. I admire and respect Audre Lorde. Her work many Black people find exceedingly difficult. And so a lot of our people are not going to buy her books. But she's an excellent poet.

BBB: What about some of the writers that came out of the sixties in terms of their production? What about Etheridge Knight?

Brooks: Etheridge Knight as you know has a new book, *Belly Song*. I admire it, I admire a good deal of it, but I prefer *Poems from Prison*.

BBB: What about Mari Evans?

Brooks: Oh yes, she's one of our best poets. She writes in a way that people who wouldn't dream of paying ten dollars for a book of poetry can relate to and would buy the book. And, she too publishes with a Black publisher, Third World Press, I believe.

BBB: What about Sonia Sanchez?

Brooks: Sonia is experimenting in feeling here and there, and I don't know just what she's going to come up with, but just now she is publishing simpler kinds of poems. She seems to be very much interested in love songs. She says that she wants to write an epic. She's good.

BBB: What about Imamu Baraka?

Brooks: I don't think that anybody can speak for him, because he changes constantly and I understand that he isn't doing much writing now. So I don't know just what his present status is.

BBB: Nikki Giovanni?

Brooks: She is young and I believe that she will have many changes in her life—I have in mine—she isn't nearly fifty-six so we'll just have to wait and see what happens in the future.

BBB: Michael Harper?

Brooks: Michael Harper is an excellent writer, and an excellent poet, one who really knows language and knows what to do with it. My favorite poem of his is, and this will tip you off I suppose to the kind of thing that I like, "The Algiers Motel Incident."

BBB: What about Ishmael Reed?

Brooks: I really don't feel qualified to say a good deal about Ishmael Reed because I haven't read much of his work. I have read some of his poetry and I consider it good. And he, too, like Michael Harper, is an excellent manipulator of language. I think that these people will be doing exciting things in the future.

BBB: Much of the major writing that came out of the sixties in terms of Black people was published first in the *Liberator*, *Soul Book*, *Black World*, *Essence*, and *Ebony*. What do you see in terms of the future of Black magazines and the media?

Brooks: You left *Journal of Black Poetry* and *Black Scholar*. These along with *Black World* and *Black Collegian*, though I haven't read *Black Collegian* for quite some time, are my favorites: Of course, everybody reads *Ebony* and what others did you mention?

BBB: *Essence, Liberator*, and *Soul Book*.

Brooks: I think everybody buys or turns over the pages of *Essence* on the stand. It is said that when *Liberator* and *Soul Book* did live that they were very important. My interest in a Black magazine is that its focus be Black and for my magazine, *The Black Position*, I'm interested in stating and featuring the Black position.

BBB: What do you think that position is? What would you say to somebody who said what do you mean by Black?

Brooks: Well, my stress is on Black unity so I favor those things that create and sustain Black unity.

BBB: When Maulana Karenga talks about Black unity, he talks about not only color but culture and consciousness. And we find today that in many cases Black people here are trying to regain their culture which gives them a sense of identity, purpose and direction. And on the other hand you find that some of the elders steadfastly stay with the old terminology. To the young, Afrikan and Black mean the same thing. And of course the older generation still uses negro. What do you say to a person who continues to use a term such as negro, which undoubtedly has been proven to many of the young to be not only disgusting but. . . .

Brooks: I agree with that. I deplore the word negro, colored and all the rest of that stuff, but when you mention the elders, may I say that many of the younger are going back to where some of us were some years ago. And I find this most upsetting. And a lot of the young women who wore naturals for many years are now straightening their hair. And many of them are using the word negro themselves. And their emphasis is on "America" and all things "American." They are interested in money and fancy clothes. I shouldn't say fancy clothes, because many of them have turned their back on anything Black and Afrikan.

BBB: You have of course me and talked with and, at one level have been friends with the last generation of writers: John Killens, James Baldwin, Margaret Danner, and Langston Hughes. For example, John O. Killens and Langston Hughes we know have helped many young writers. Could you comment on your association with Langston Hughes?

Brooks: I met Langston Hughes when I was sixteen. When I went to Metropolitan Community Church to show him some of my poems at the behest of my mother who accompanied me and saw to it that I did this. He was most kind and read the poems right there after his reading and told me that I had talent and that I should keep writing. Later I met him again because he came to a poetry workshop that a reader on the staff of *Poetry Magazine* had started at the Southside Community Art Center. Her name was Inez Cunningham Stark. And he attended one of the meetings. People who belonged to this group were Bill Couch, Margaret Burroughs, Fem Gayden, Margaret Cunningham, who is now Margaret Danner, and Edward Bland. Langston Hughes was mostly excited about the work that we were reading and he predicted a beautiful future for all of us. Later on still I gave a party for him when I lived at 623 Sixty-third Street and there were about seventy-five people or so crowded into our little two room kitchenette, and nobody had a better time then Langston Hughes who was real "folk." Never any airs or pomposities from him. And as you say, he has helped a great many young people. Showing interest in their work and encouraging them.

BBB: Many young writers see you as you saw Langston Hughes, in terms of giving direction and aiding in many ways, in terms of helping them get published and financially also. Do you think that this is the role of the elder writer in relationship to the younger writer?

Brooks: I certainly do. I think that this should be their prime function other than their writing. I think that a writer as old as myself in spite of early difficulties has had time to achieve, if there is going to be any achievement. It's hard for youngsters coming along to gain exposure, sometimes just to eat.

BBB: But it was hard for you, too. It wasn't an easy trail to where you are now. And it is still not easy.

Brooks: Well as far as eating was concerned, I must give my husband credit who had a hard time supporting his family for over twenty years. I mean that was the only place that money was coming from. And it was very hard for him.

BBB: In that respect, what do you think about the women's liberation movement?

Brooks: I've been on panels with a good many of the women's libbers and I'm very disturbed by the fact that so many of them seem to despise men, really seem to hate men. And for Black women to hate Black men is contradictory to what we are about. And I don't want to see our Black women going that route. I don't like this nose thumbing at Black men. I think that that's another divisionary tactic that we need to be very wary of. We should be about *Black liberation*—which includes women and men.

BBB: Why do you live in Chicago? Why not Miami or the West Coast? Why did you choose Chicago?

Brooks: I didn't choose Chicago, but I've grown up here and just stayed in the neighborhood that is familiar. When I got to Dar Es Salaam, I got so excited about the beauty there, that I had the idea of being around layers and layers of Black people that I thought of getting a house there, but I don't know how practical that would be. I think that there is plenty of work for me to do right here because there are plenty of Black people here. Well, here I am today. Things may change tomorrow, but I am here today.

BBB: Are you satisfied with your life as it stands now?

Brooks: No, who could be satisfied with my production and the way we are treated in this country. But the last thing in the world I intend to do is to imitate other people's way of writing, but I would be much happier if I had written poems that *so* many black people found relevant. I'm not happy about the things that are going on in this world. But I do whatever I can to rectify what I see as rectifiable. All my energy and resources will be used for the benefit of my people.

BBB: Many people feel that your work is much more political now, which I would argue with because I think that it has always been political because it positively dealt with Black people. I think that everything is political but some people feel that your work is much more distinguishably "Black" and therefore makes it that much more political.

Brooks: Well, isn't that interesting that to be Black is to be political. That word doesn't bother me either. I don't sit down and say, well today I'm going to write a political poem and it will scare all the whites. I don't have that in my mind at all. I really believe what the young said—that Black poetry is written by Blacks, about Blacks, to Blacks—and that is really all that I have in my mind.

BBB: I would leave the phrase that Chancellor Williams emphasized and that is *Black unity*. I think that that should be our flag. The unity of Black people is the *only* way I see of saving the Black race and the reason Chancellor Williams book, *The Destruction of Black Civilization*, is not in the best seller's list is because he points out in very clear terms what Black people should be doing for our survival. Read the chapter "A View from the Bridge" in the revised edition. Thank you, Gwen.

Brooks: It is I who should be thanking you.

Update on Part One: An Interview with Gwendolyn Brooks

Gloria T. Hull and Posey Gallagher / 1977

From *CLA Journal* 21, 1 (Sept. 1977), 19–40. Reprinted by permission of the College Language Association.

Hull: I would like to begin by asking you to assess your new direction (since 1968). One of the things which you always state is that you want to develop a new Gwendolynian voice, a "newish" kind of voice. How would you say that this "newish" voice of yours is working out?

Brooks: Very gradually. I want to write poetry that will appeal to many, many blacks, not just the blacks who go to college but also those who have their customary habitat in taverns and the street—people who have grown up feeling that poetry was not for them, but who are able to enjoy poetry if it seems to them relevant to what they know of life.

Hull: You've been saying that for how many years now—four or five? I know you said that same thing in *Report from Part One*.

Brooks: Yes, it was published in 1972; and I am still struggling. I haven't written *anything* yet that seems to be just the kind of thing I want to achieve. I want it to be song-like in nature, something that can easily be transported from one person to another with enjoyment. It's a *very* difficult task. Other people have achieved this for themselves (not anything I can model myself after). For example, Sonia Sanchez is able to speak her poetry to all kinds of blacks and be eagerly, nourishingly received. So can Haki, but he himself is experimenting in different ways now. And he seems to be interested in writing something that's a little closer to some of the things that I used to be warned against.

Hull: What have you written that approximates most closely what you're trying to achieve? You say you haven't quite gotten to it yet; but what's the closest thing to it?

Brooks: I can't say complete poems except perhaps for "We Real Cool," and I can't write a thousand "We Real Cool"'s.

Hull: Furthermore, you wrote that before you began your new program.
Brooks: Yes, interesting.

Hull: So since you've consciously had this as your aim, what do you think approximates what you're striving for?

Brooks: There are some struggles toward it in the little book *Beckonings*, in a poem like "The Boy Died in My Alley" and yet that leads toward the traditional, almost irresistibly, in several parts. The rhyming there, too, and the very close rhythm is not something that I'm considering proper to my new yearning.

Hull: When you say it's traditional, do you mean that it's the rhyme and the close rhythm that smacks of the traditional?

Brooks: Not only that. Toward the end of the poem I like the way it rises up. (I guess this is the old me so far as that appreciation goes.) But that is the kind of thing—though it is not involved language—that I could hardly take into a tavern and get a proper response to.

Hull: So, that poem comes closest to being what you want to write even though there at the end it doesn't exactly satisfy you?

Brooks: Some of the ordinariness of the language is also suitable to my new idea, my new compulsion.

Hull: Do you think that you are a poet of ordinary language and, as you said someplace, of ordinary speech, loose rhythm and human talk because you get some of your best effects by coming up with the unusual word in just the right place. Do you think that that's your poetic bent?

Brooks: What you're implying is something that, if true, is probably very sad because you are probably saying without even knowing it or knowing it and accepting limitations in me. You may be saying that I cannot hope to be the kind of poet who can walk into a tavern and gather them all into me in a matter of a few words. I happen to think, however, that the valid poem that I want to write (because it will probably have valid itemata) can be significant for the unique word and still be accessible to all manner of life. I think that is something that I will have to keep on trying for. It might be better if I wrote more story poems because everybody loves a story. Story, I should keep in mind; music, I should keep in mind; and brevity perhaps. There really isn't a lot of patience with a *long, long, long poem* especially if it has a lot of complication. So I won't give up, Gloria! But you're right. It's taken a long time and I still haven't reached it yet.

Hull: I know what you want to reach but there's such a dichotomy between what I call your distinctive Gwendolyn Brooks style and what you're trying for. I can tell there's a transition because in looking at *Beckonings*, I see the dual impulses at work.

Brooks: I do, too. *Beckonings* is the great failure among all of my books, but I don't feel unhappy about having brought it out. Unlike dear Ralph Ellison whom I admire, AD-Mire, I'm not scared to bring out things that just might be far less than my standards. And I agree with you: that is a book which shows dual impulses struggling. Maybe the next book will be better. I hope so.

Hull: When you're trying for ordinary speech, loose rhythms and accessibility, what happens is that many poems turn out like ballads—for example, "The Boy Died in My Alley". . . .

Brooks:. . . and "Steam Song." Possibly it's over-simple. There's something else wrong with that poem that I meant to mention to somebody. There is something that bothers me about it and I'm sure it bothers other women—where I say, "My man is my only necessary thing." I don't believe that. (Of course, I'm not necessarily supposed to be the speaker, but people will assume that I am). I do not believe that a man is a woman's only *necessary* thing—for heaven's sake! That's one I let slip by me.

Hull: Would you say that *Beckonings* represents where you are poetically right now?

Brooks: Maybe so—with all its failures. Yes, I guess so. You know I rarely look over my own things, but the other day I did. A lot of what I have written (even though it does not answer my present needs) I feel okay about. Now that doesn't mean I think that any poem, ANY poem is perfect. But I do stop short of improving things once they're published.

Hull: Since you mention looking over your own work, are you sure that your early poems are, in fact, so inaccessible? I think not. Furthermore, should taveneers *be* the standard for your poetry? Should you use them as your reference point—rather than, say, people in church or people like us who can appreciate your more imagistic, more demanding work?

Brooks: George Kent, my biographer, agrees with you that I should not be overly concerned about this. He thinks I should continue to write as I have been writing. He also doesn't have much sympathy with my constant announced concerns for the taverneers. However, I feel that I was right when in the late sixties, I believed that blacks should care for each other, nourish each other and communicate with each other. And if that was the right decision, I cannot forget the people who have grown up feeling that they hate poetry; that they would spell the word with a capital P and look upon it with great awe. I feel that there are poems that those people could enjoy. There are already some and I would like to contribute to this literature which, if they knew it was called literature, they would probably turn away from.

Hull: In terms of trying to satisfy those taveneers who are one segment, as well as continue to be the kind of poet that you are, sometimes it looks as if you are trying to do two things that you may not be able to pull together in a way which will satisfy both motivations and impulses.

Brooks: I think they have been pulled together—those dual impulses—in the work of other poets. I have mentioned Robert Burns who seems to me to write poetry that is quickly accessible and still manages to have it called literature by people who feel that they know what literature is.

Hull: Think about things like what you can do with diction and language, richness of imagery, and imaginativeness of comparison.

Brooks: I believe all those elements can be included in a ballad that people who feel they despise poetry will not have to struggle over. I believe unique expressions can be used in a quotes, "simple poem." You just need a couple of unique expressions to distinguish a simple poem, to lift it up.

Hull: But there's no where that you've done this?

Brooks: The one poem I can keep recalling is "We Real Cool," but I almost hate to recall it though because I wrote ten poems that sounded like "We Real Cool," "We Real Cool" would lose whatever effectiveness it has. I guess I haven't, Gloria.

Hull: Why do you think you haven't since you know what needs to be done and you think it's really possible. Maybe we're underestimating the task. . . .

Brooks: And maybe we are also underestimating what I have achieved along these lines—or maybe I am because earlier I mentioned even such a longish, but successful, poem as "The Ballad of Pearl May Lee." A lot has to do with the subject matter. I have to tackle some subjects that will seem relevant to these people that I keep favoring—SAVORY. And I can certainly say there is always a lot of response to "Pearl May Lee" especially among white men and black women. And of course people always like love poems. Another poem I can read in a tavern is "when you have forgotten Sunday" and "Steam Song" (which is not one of my favorites). These are poems where people can say "Yeah, I've had that feeling myself." Another one of my problems, Gloria, is that I'm not as prolific as I used to be. Part of that is laziness and part of that is fear—not the Ellisonian fear of coming below your standards but of not being able to achieve what I want to do here—this urge of mine to write poems that will appeal to people who quotes, "don't like poetry."

Hull: That's interesting because developing this style probably involves experimentation. You're probably more likely to get to it if you just keep writing.

Brooks: That fights with my compulsion not to write at *all* unless I'm really hotly inspired. (I'm not scared of the word "inspiration.") I get an idea and get all excited about it and have to put down notes and presently have to come back and revise. Of late I've been making lots and lots of notes. I expect to do a considerable amount of writing this summer.

Hull: Just one more question and then we'll leave the subject of *Beckonings* and "The Program." Are all of the poems that are in *Beckonings* recent ones? Were they all written within two or three years prior to their publication in 1975?

Brooks: I think so. Let's say they were all seventies poems.

Hull: Let's talk a little bit now about your ideas in regard to blackness and where we are in 1977. You mentioned a falling away. How do you feel about that falling away? Has it caused you to wonder about the tenacity with which you are "holding"?

Brooks: I couldn't believe that women were going to straighten their hair again. I guess I was a fool, must have been. I was just amazed when I saw that coming back. It just seemed a deliberate self-slap in the face. They all look—and I don't mind saying it—they all look UN-NATURAL to me. Now of course those who just naturally have unnatural hair can't help that. Now, I may seem to be giving too much attention to that but I believe that it's a symbol of where we are now, that we have so little pride as to feel that other people's hair is more beautiful than ours and to deliberately go out and imitate it. That nice togethery-ness that was developing, a lot of us are losing. Once again we're emphasizing the individual, loving self above the group. I thought maybe *Roots* would bring some of the pride back and it has seemed to have a good effect, but already people are starting to jump on Alex Haley for this and that. As I told my husband, I think a lot of that is organized. I really do. They don't want that book and the things that he has to say to be over-favored, oversubscribed to.

Hull: So you see all of that as subversive and organized resistance to going back to feelings that were more prevalent in the late sixties?

Brooks: I'm not crazy; I don't feel we can "go back." I think some of the best parts that happened then should be carried forward into the future to be used. And warmth among blacks is a positive; hatred among blacks is a negative. A lot of us hate ourselves. We're going off in this direction or that direction and we're doing everything except (I don't care how mushy it sounds), loving each other. We want to be like the big white man on Park Avenue. However, I see signs that blacks are turning toward each other and beginning to continue a belief in themselves and in their future. I attribute this, to some extent, to *Roots* and to the uprisings in Africa. Also, on college campuses, I'm detecting an impatience with just being passive.

Hull: When you sit down to write poetry by, about and to blacks, does something essentially different happen than when you sat down to write *A Street in Bronzeville* or *In the Mecca*?

Brooks: Not essentially. First of all, I don't sit down and say, "I am now going to write a poem by, about and to all blacks." I am myself. I am consumed with the passion of ideas that I came to believe in in the late sixties. They are now built into myself. I am THAT—so anything that I write is going to issue from a concern with and interest in blackness and its progress. Now that can include a funny poem, an entertaining poem, a love poem of joy of living poem. When my husband and I (my husband doesn't see everything the way I do) were in Ghana we would have some fierce arguments (he calls them discussions). Once we were walking down a road and we saw a little Ghanaian boy. He was running and happy in the happy sunshine. My husband made a comment springing from an argument we had had the night before that lasted until four in the morning. He said, "Now look, see that little boy. That is a perfect picture of happy youth. So if you were writing a poem about him, why couldn't you just let it go at that? Write a poem about running boy-happy, happy-running boy?" That's the kind of poem he said he would write if he were writing about this boy. He would just see him not as a black boy but as youth-happy. So I said if you wrote exhaustively about running boy and you noticed that the boy was black, you would have to go further than a celebration of blissful youth. You just might consider that when a black boy runs, maybe not in Ghana, but perhaps on the Chicago South

Side, you'd have to remember a certain friend of my daughter's in high school—beautiful boy, so smart, one of the honor students, and just an all-around fine young fellow. He was running down an alley with a friend of his, just running and a policeman said "Halt!" And before he could slow up his steps, he just shot him. Now that happens all the time in Chicago. There was all that promise in a little crumpled heap. Dead forever. So I would have to think about that in a poem I was writing about a running boy.

What I was going to tell you earlier—very briefly—is this. My daughter was enacting a street scene about her peers. The subject was a young black fellow who was real—what do you people say these days?—who was real hip. That's not your word now—he was GETTIN DOWN! I admired it and I said, "I don't think I can write a novel that would be inclusive in the way that your little skit is." So my husband said, "Oh, that's all right, Gwen (I thought he was praising me at first), write your kind of novel—IGNORE LIFE!" He was joking (in a way) and in a way the part of it that was not a joke was justified because there *is* a lot I cannot get into my pages. I'll see what I can do, though. I'm going to bring Maud Martha up to my age. There is a lot I can say and a lot I can't say.

Hull: Give us a little of the plot, starting with her pregnancy with her second child.

Brooks: Well, she has that child and she has another child and then her husband dies in the bus fire that happened in Chicago in the fifties. One of those flammable trucks with a load of oil ran into a street car and about thirty-six people burned right out on Sixty-third and State Streets. So I put her husband in that fire. Wasn't that nice of me? I have taken him as far as I could. He certainly wasn't going to change. I could see that.

Hull: Is that why you kill him in the novel?

Brooks: I had planned to go ahead and write more, but I wanted Maud Martha to have additional adventures. She will probably get involved with another man up the way but I would like to wait until she is almost my age, certainly fifty.

Hull: So Maud is a mother alone raising her three children. Then what happens?

Brooks: Well, that chapter ends with her feeling, at the moment, a certain unbidden relief. She indicates that those little feelings that she'll have of intense regret when she perhaps opens up a drawer and sees some little me-

mento of the past have not hit her yet. Right now, coming back from the funeral, she's thinking passionately about the cake that's going to be at the wake and how good it's going to be.

Hull: What are some of the adventures that you foresee her having?

Brooks: Well, I want her to go to Africa. I haven't figured out how she's going to get there but she's going to be involved with youth as I am. (You know I have a club on my street of high school students.) For some reason, she will decide that she's got to do everything she can for them. Now her resources are going to be slender. So, how does she get to Africa? I haven't worked that out yet. Something will come along that will give her that opportunity and her expenses will be paid. Maybe she'll be chosen as a guide to accompany a bunch of kids that somebody who's crazy like myself has sponsored.

Hull: You're apparently putting a lot of yourself into the sequel of *Maud Martha.*

Brooks: Yes, I will, as I did with *Maud Martha.* That has much autobiography though I've twisted things.

Hull: Will it be the same kind of incorporation of self with a twisting? How will it differ?

Brooks: Well, I expect to use more of my imagination.

Hull: Will it be less directly autobiographical than the original *Maud Martha?*

Brooks: I really can't guarantee you what it will be.

Hull: Can you say if it will be written in the same style—the short chapters and very poetic prose?

Brooks: Oh yes, it will be even shorter.

Hull; When do you think you're going to have that done?

Brooks: Within three years—don't look so amazed, that's not a long time!

Hull: It seems as if it is for somebody like me who's been waiting.——— You talked earlier about the way you write your poetry. Is it still the same as when you first started writing? Do you find now that you polish more, polish less; revise more, revise less; write more on the fly or need more concentration or what?

Brooks: I revise as much as I ever did. I still bend intently over the little phrase, as I said in "In the Mecca."

Hull: Did you bend as intently over the phrases in, for example, "The Boy Died in My Alley" as you did over "In the Mecca?"

Brooks: I tried to, but then that was a different kind of poem. I was also trying to be quotes, "simple." I didn't worry about that when I was writing "In the Mecca."

Hull: It seems that if what you're trying to do is to be simpler. . . .

Brooks: . . . it's even harder to accomplish because I don't want to write sloppily. I want to see that every word does its job just as I did before.

Hull: Among the other projects you want to pursue at some point, you mentioned verse plays. What is happening with these plays?

Brooks: I haven't done anything of that sort yet. Someday I would like to write a little book of a few verse plays that would be chiefly for reading. I've never been good with plot. So I don't think I could carry it off as a play that would be exciting to look at on stage, but I'd like it to be something meditative, ruminative that could be read with lively dialogue. . . .

Hull: Any idea of subject?

Brooks: It could be any subject that's happening today.

Hull: How near are you to doing an update on the autobiography?

Brooks: I just might begin some little something this summer but I don't think it ought to come out right away. I think I ought to give myself the chance to be in the midst of more happenings.

Hull: You mention somewhere that you do want to bring it up to date because there have been many changes since then. What are some of the changes that you would want to speak about in that autobiography?

Brooks: Well, my observation about some of what we've mentioned here. I would certainly make some lively comments about, for example, a move in this country to send blacks to Africa to kill other blacks. A step like that would interest me very much and I'd be interested to see if blacks would let themselves be sent over there to kill their brothers and sisters. Some of them would—so I would write about. . . .

Hull: All of that is more or less commentary on worldly conditions, but a great deal of what is valuable in *Report from Part One* is the knowledge it provides about you. You, I think, are a very reticent person and have the nicest way I know of finessing personal questions into something else.

Brooks: You say I'm reticent? How can you say that? It seems to me that I'm always spilling out.

Hull: But it's not really personal.

Brooks: Well what kind of *personalness* do you want? I could talk about my club—which is my main interest these days. Really, there isn't a lot of personal stuff going on in my life. There has been, but the time for writing about that has passed (if there ever was a time for writing about it and I'm not going to write about it now).

Hull: Do you mean since 1972 or before 1972?

Brooks: Before 1972 and after 1972?

Hull: So you do not foresee having anything in there. . . .

Brooks: . . . HOT! Ain't gone be *nothing hot*! The only thing that I could record is that my husband and I went back together—which most people would not see as particularly hot. I would update things on that score by saying that we went back together and telling how it happened.

Hull: Give us a preview.

Brooks: Well, my mother has always favored our marriage. And when her eighty-fifth birthday came, I did everything I could to make that day memorable for her. So I decided to call my husband and tell him about her birthday and ask him—as a surprise—if he would join us for dinner. He said he would be perfectly delighted to. As we talked, he told me about the poetry he had been writing. He recited some of the poems and they were really good. I said, "Those poems have *got* to be published." Then, afterwards, he said he would like to take me out to dinner and we would talk some more about these poems. So we did that—and talked about poetry and that's the way it happened. We just finally got back together—went to London for a sort of second honeymoon (never did have a first one). We had a good time. All in all, I would say it was the quotes, "right thing" to do.

Remember I told you about companionship. Well, that *is* important. It is like my poem "Shorthand Possible." I mentioned being able to say just a few words and whole troops of memories come back. That's one of the nicest things about being married. Then, too, we have the kids in common.

Hull: But they're grown.

Brooks: No, you can't say that; that's a family unit. There are just so many memories involved with the children. For instance, when they come, there's real happiness in the dining room. They're bouncing things back and forth. (All of them are great wits.) Stuff will just be scissoring and knifing past me. Sometimes I pick it up and sometimes I don't, but it's all a very nice thing.

Hull: Speaking on the subject of marriage, you mention in *Part One* that in marriage, especially if you are a woman, you are always "setting yourself aside constantly." And you said that you wanted solitude and liked to be able to control your own life. Is this passage from *Part One* really the way you feel about marriage?

Brooks: Well, I can't say that is something that is general for every woman, especially these days. I imagine fewer and fewer women are content to set themselves aside.

Gallagher: I'm surprised you keep such an optimistic outlook towards marriage, especially since you've said that you enjoyed your freedom.

Brooks: That has nothing to do with my observation of marriage quotes, "in the long run." I don't expect a young woman to really enter into my feelings about it because young women are, and are properly so, determined to have everything right. And I believe every young woman ought to start out with that intention. It takes many years before you realize that nothing is going to be flawless. You put the positives over here and the negatives over there, and if the positives are bulkier than the negatives, you go with them. And it's really beautiful—this steady companionship—having somebody you can talk things over with, whom you're known so long that you can count on certain responses.

Hull: Do you consider yourself a professional poet?

Brooks: I see myself as being a very open writer. In fact, that's the very essence of writing as far as I'm concerned. Many of my poems—love poems and others—are autobiographical. You speak of things you know, things you feel, things you have personally observed. (Observation I feel is an aspect of experience.) You'll find my personal interpretation of hundreds of things that are life things. *Maud Martha* is heavily autobiographical. I've twisted many things and actually used my imagination here and there. But take a chapter like "A Birth," that is, with maybe only one change I can think of, a report of the birth of my first child. The change is that I made a baby a girl instead of a boy.

Hull: Let me ask you two different, related questions. What else do you yet have to say in your poetry that you or anyone else has not said? And how would you evaluate your work over the years? Do you think it's improving. When was/is your best period? What do you think is your best work?

Brooks: I think the best way to answer that is to go back to the books starting with the first one and tell you what I think of each. I think that *A Street in Bronzeville* was the book that most people including myself will feel cozier in. It's a folksy book and it's full of people and story. I like that and most people like those qualities in a book of poetry. *Annie Allen* is a book of extensive experiment. In writing that book I didn't always have the best motives. I wanted to *prove* that I could write well. I didn't go to the extent that Melvin Tolson did but I enjoyed being technically passionate. It did result in some rather artificial poetry. I think the "Anniad" is just an exercise, just an exercise.

Hull: But it has good lines.

Brooks: Yes, it does have good lines. That's about what it is—a collection of occurrences, many occurrences, I would say, of good lines. But it's nothing for anyone to treasure or be nourished by. (I like that word "nourish." There are some poems in there that I do like, that I enjoyed writing—for example, the sonnets though I keep saying—and I believe it's true—that I won't be writing other sonnets.

Hull: So what do you feel is your best work?

Brooks: I think I ought to go on telling you how I feel about these books. I'm glad they're all together in *The World* of because there's something to recommend each other—in my terms. Other people might say the whole batch is disposable—but I'm not prepared to say that.) *The Bean Eaters* has been called a political work. I'm impatient with that use of the word political. But it does show a growing concern with what's happening all around us of social concern. And there are some poems in there that I would be unwilling to have removed from my final collection such as the Mississippi mother poem and "Lovers of the Poor." It always surprises me when I remember that "We Real Cool" is in there. I keep thinking that it came earlier. Then *In the Mecca* is again an effort at doing something different. I'm glad I wrote it though it is not successful in the way I wanted it to be. For one thing, I wanted it to be much longer—two thousand lines; it didn't even get to a thousand, and then there are other poems in there that suggest I have an interest in things that I have an interest in today—"The Blackstone Rangers" for example.

Hull: Did you write *In the Mecca* at the same time?
Brooks: No!

Hull: Are there parts that were later interpolated? I'm thinking particularly about "Way-Out Morgan" and the "Don Lee wants" part. Did you stick those parts in?
Brooks: There is a little ballad in there, "The Ballad of Edie Barrow" which I wrote long, long, long ago. That was the only odd piece. "Way-Out Morgan" I wrote along as I was writing the poem. It wasn't "stuck in." Don Lee's poem *was* added *because* I wanted to get his name in there. He seemed to me to be—and still does seem to be—an influence of that time that needed to be registered. But most of that poem was written straight along. "Riot" was really an effort at communication with a lot of people. I didn't succeed except in patches. It too is meditative. After that, "Family Pictures" which I think is a good little collection. Some of it veers into pedestrianism but for what it was supposed to be it pretty much comes off, I think. I like the "Young Heroes" and it has "The Life of Lincoln West" which I wrote however back in '53 or '54. Then came "Aloneness." I really don't know what to say about it except that it is something I wanted to say.

Hull: So, are you suggesting that there isn't a period you would consider your best?
Brooks: I like something from each.

Hull: Do you think your work is improving steadily?
Brooks: No, I think this is true for a lot of writers and certainly for myself. You go back and forth. Sometimes you're writing well as You see it and sometimes you're not. And writing well right now for me is writing effectively in the terms I have stated for you. And we all agree that I'm not doing that yet, so how can I consider this present stage successful? It's a groping stage.

Hull: How did you respond to my question, what else do you yet have to say in your poetry that you or anyone else hasn't said?
Brooks: Oh nothing that no one else has said. I don't worry about such things. Why should I aim to do something nobody else has done? It will be mine if I do it right.

Hull: What do you feel that you still have to or want to say?
Brooks: I want to write about all aspects of the black experience which again will not always be a preaching kind of thing, just being a reporter.

Hull: Do you think that you'll start bringing out bigger books again instead of the small pamphlets?

Brooks: Lord, if I could just bring out a *small* book that satisfies me, I would be happy! I think it's wonderful, though, that this is a paperback time. That was another thing about the 60's—people did start to bring out just a few poems and I thought that was good.

Gallagher: Could you talk a little bit about the poets who have reverted to the way you were writing prior to the late sixties?

Brooks: I wouldn't trouble to name any of them. But it's enough to say that some of them wrote rather rowdily then and used four letter words. Now, some are writing very carefully polished poetry in forms, even haiku.

Hull: Do you think it's wrong, or deplorable, or less than desirable that these poets are now writing as you're trying to stop writing? I think it's a fine irony.

Brooks: I think it's a stage. I think they're going to change again.

Hull: And do what?

Brooks: I don't know. Perhaps go on from where they came from with a little less rawness maybe but still not so much finesse.

Hull: Might not their beginning to write with some of this finesse be perceived as growth in the same way as your beginning to write in another style?

Brooks: Not when it tends to obscurity.

Hull: Is that what's happening?

Brooks: With some of it.

Hull: Why is it that more of your earlier poems deal with female characters and the sequences of women's lives, but now you don't have as many such poems? Think, for instance, about *A Street in Bronzeville* and all of *Annie Allen*. This is not to say that your earlier works don't have men too, but there is a relative absence of women-centered poems in your later work.

Brooks: Oh, is that true? I have to listen to you because I really haven't thought about these things—except about the first question: some women have told me that I have written a lot of "women poems." I checked at that time and saw that I did have more poems about women than I had thought. But I didn't know there was a peak out.

Hull: Look at *A Street in Bronzeville*: "The Mother," "Hunchback Girl," "A Song in the Front Yard," "Chocolate Mabie," "Sadie and Maud," "the

Hattie Scott" series, and the entire book of *Annie Allen*. Then in *The Bean Eaters* there is "Old Mary," "Bronzeville Mother," "The Crazy Woman," and so on. There are also some in *In the Mecca*. But, then, when you look at your later works, many of the poems are written to men: Medgar Evers, Malcolm X, and the Blackstone Rangers. You write to John Oliver Killens and Don L. Lee. I'm speaking generally about your later work now where the kind of black women's experience that you deal with earlier, you're not writing about anymore. The figures that you're focusing on are male.

Brooks: I don't know how to account for that. When I talk about young heroes, I mention Walter Bradford who had a high influence on my life. He was the one whom Oscar Brown put me in touch with because he was a teenage organizer and knew the Rangers. He helped round them up for me. He and Haki are equal in my estimate. They are, in a way, sons of mine. I've even written about this but never did publish it although I will sometime. We still think of ourselves as mother and sons. And they have been more like sons to me than my own son because they have ideas that are like my own. And they have just been more the way a mother dreams of—affectionate, and we have a sharing of ideas. So it's only natural that I have written a good deal about them. these people who influenced me so much in the late sixties tended to be men. When I had this workshop, it was the men who usually set out ideas to be examined. The women—what can I say about them? For instance, when we dedicated "The Wall," the men organized the whole thing. I don't know. . . . Have I written any poems to the women? Did I write a poem to Carolyn Rodgers?

Hull: The best I can help you out with is to recall that you give Val a nice section in the Wall poem when you call her a little black stampede. But otherwise *no—no*, I'm sorry.

Brooks: Well what were the women doing, Gloria, aside from amending what the others did? I could write some poems now about Val's Kuumba workshop, which had been very influential in Chicago. I could do a little series of poems about her experiences there. I haven't chiefly because I've been busy with other things and because of laziness. I have also written a little prose tribute to Carolyn which I will be publishing.

Hull: What comes to my mind is what people like Sonia Sanchez and others said about black women being told to take a back seat at that time. Maybe it only stands to reason that your concept of late-sixties blackness would be male-identified?

Brooks: I have to be very careful that you aren't putting any words into my mouth and mind. At least that wasn't a conscious decision. I didn't say, "Okay, women are supposed to take the back seat and I won't write about them." I nodded during what you said because it certainly was true that on account of everything that had been done to smash our men down there was this tendency on the part of the women—announced too—to lift men up to *heroize* them.

Hull: I guess what I'm saying is I see you doing that same thing in your poetry and I would like to see the other side too which you have written so movingly about.

Brooks: You're right to want to see the other side. It's a legitimate complaint.

Hull: Well, what about the private experience of black women, what I think Haki calls the "black womanness" in your poems. That is private experience and you don't write poems like that any more either.

Brooks: I don't write about private experience? Why, I think that most of my poems extend from privacies. Something that has happened to me will often find its way into a poem. I don't always say that it's my own experience but I wonder just how necessary that is.

Hull: What I mean are poems related to women's lives, poems like the abortion poem, the Hattie Scott poems, the hair-dresser poems, "A Sunset of the City." Those are excellent examples of what I mean. Can you speculate about why you don't write that kind of poem anymore?

Brooks: Now, I see what you mean. I just have not had any inspiration for that kind of poem of late. I don't know. What does it indicate about the turn my life is taking? What does it mean—because I'm still a woman? It's interesting and I'm glad you brought it up because it's a subject I've never mulled over. I was excited and interested when those women said to me, "You've written a lot of women poems." They apparently hadn't gotten to *In the Mecca* because they didn't notice that they began to dwindle.

Hull: They were seeing you in toto and in toto it *is* true that you have.

Brooks: Well that's interesting. You've really enlarged my own vision of myself because I've never said any of the things I've said to you in a desperate attempt to understand why men came to the fore in my poetry in the late sixties. I hadn't even thought about it but it is try. It is true. And this afternoon will have a bearing on my future. Seriously, because I too feel that it's a very bad omission—and especially in times when women are really rousing themselves and doing some fiery things, and even more than that, thinking fiery things. So, we'll see. But then, *Maud Martha* is coming up and that will be another woman statement.

Hull: Oh, yes. You can see why we all have you identified with making that kind of woman statement. But you can also see where that falls in terms of chronology.

Brooks: Yes, I do see. Interesting. Would you say that the late sixties was a male time?

Hull: Not inherently so, although many black men did fall into this white women's role thing.

Brooks: You're absolutely right about that. I remember that when Haki was working with Baraka, they were both very first about men being the leaders. The women assisted. They worked hard, very hard. In fact, there was a lot of talk then about those three steps behind and many young black women never liked that at all. Yes, you're absolutely right and I'm glad that we're talking in this way.

Hull: That's the whole context from which I'm pursuing this question with you because you can't succomb to that too.

Brooks: You're right. You're right.

Hull: Being close to Haki and knowing Baraka, how do you feel about that?

Brooks: Well, Haki has changed now in so far as I can see. His outfit has held to all the original ideas except that one.

Hull: In closing, let me ask you a few miscellaneous questions. At a convention which I recently attended, it was announced that some group of people who had been polled determined that you and Robert Hayden were the two greatest living Afro-American poets. Do you agree with this assessment and what do you think about his poetry? Can you compare and contrast yourself with Hayden?

Brooks: I think he's a more careful writer than I am. He has been more interested in technical ways of doing things than I have been. And of course the great difference in the two of us as black people is that in the late sixties I was highly excited by and in favor of the "wild little boys and girls" who were writing "all that poetry." I don't know how he feels about them now (he may have reassessed their accomplishments), but he did not have much faith in their ability as poets. He is a Bahai too—which is another difference. I don't have any special religion. My religion is—I guess I'll say something corny—PEOPLE. LIV—ING. I go to church on Mother's Day and Easter Sunday. I will say, however, that when I'm up in a plane and lately when I'm in a car or any other conveyance I say Dear—please protect us all—and then sit back and enjoy the ride.

Hull: Do you see any similarities in your work and Hayden's work?

Brooks: He's a better technician than I am and more dedicated. What I'm saying is that we can be compared in our interest in technique. And of course we are both interested in blacks being justly treated.

Hull: I would like to ask you a few questions about specific poems. Do the lines "First fight, Then fiddle" from *Annie Allen* and "Conduct your blooming in the noise and whip of the whirlwind" from *In the Mecca* mean the same thing?

Brooks: No. That mother is making the statement that such children as she has—black, deprived, disadvantaged and besieged—will have to give their attention to civilizing a space for themselves to survive in before they give their attention to such a lovely thing as the fiddling next to them. Her very use of the word "fiddle" is supposed to be significant. Of course I have transferred her thoughts into my own language. Annie Allen may or may not have spoken in that way. As I created her, I don't think she would have said that stuff that is in the sonnets—"crust, renewals." In fact, I don't talk that way myself.

Hull: And that "conduct you blooming in the noise and whip of the whirl-wind"? You may as well gloss those lines, too.

Brooks: That is quite a general statement, something that anyone can take comfort from and use. And it simply means what it says. There is a whirl-wind. Thee world is a whirlwind. The social world is a whirlwind. And what do we do? Do we tell ourselves that we'll wait until it's all over and every-thing is peaceful and loving? We might be waiting in vain. We don't know when things are going to quotes "get better"—and we don't seem inclined to force them to be better. So we see to it that we bloom, that we attend to our growth in spite of the awful things that are happening.

Hull: Can you talk about the poem "Friends" in *Beckonings*? What in-spired it?

Brooks: Oh, yes. That is something that I often speak of in addressing young women. I say that often your love affairs are going to come to an end. But what I wish for women is that they can make a friend out of a man who has been a lover. There had to be something there. After all, you are a worthwhile woman and you wouldn't take on a man who had no qualities at all.

Hull: That's the poem that you have the worksheet for, that you wrote in some hotel. . . .

Brooks: Oh, yes—and don't think that hasn't been mentioned!

Hull: It *was* rather awful! Is that draft typical of the way you write your poems? Is there usually that much dross attached to the gem of a poem which emerges?

Brooks: Let's be really frank. The whole poem itself is not a great thing, but it was a very personal statement. I thought it was something that would be relevant to a lot of women—maybe men too. (Yes, men have liked it.) But it's really not a well-written poem. As a rule I usually don't have as much absolute, utter nonsense even in a first draft as I had there. I look at that and I say "Good night! I shouldn't have given that as an example"—though it might give hope to some writers.

Hull: I was terribly fascinated by that because it was the first rough draft of yours I'd ever seen. I think you should include more of it in your *Report from Part Two*.

Brooks: That's an idea. I've got a lot of them.

Hull: In closing, is there anything you want to say or add to what we've already covered?

Brooks: I can't think of a thing. You have utterly drained me. I don't know what else I *could* say. Finis.

Interview with Gwendolyn Brooks

Claudia Tate / 1983

From *Black Women Writers at Work* by Claudia Tate (New York: Continuum Press, 1983), 39–48. Reprinted by permission of Claudia Tate.

Claudia Tate: You place your work into two distinct categories, pre-1967 and post-1967. Would you reconstruct the events of 1967, the year of transition?

Gwendolyn Brooks: In 1967 I met some "new black people" who seemed very different from youngsters I had been encountering in my travels to various college campuses. I'd been meeting some rather sleepy, unaware young people. I'm sorry to say many young people are now returning to that old sleepiness but with a difference. I have more hope for them now than I used to have because I cannot see us going back to the temper of the fifties. After what happened in the late sixties, I just can't see us crawling. But I'm getting ahead of myself. I met some of these young people at a black writers' conference at Fisk University in 1967. They seemed proud and so committed to their own people. I was fascinated by them. I returned to Chicago, still going over what they had said to me. The poets among them felt that black poets should write as blacks, about blacks, and address themselves to blacks. I had never thought deliberately in such terms. Now if you look at some of my older works, you'll see that they seem to suggest I might have had that model in mind. But I wasn't writing consciously with the idea that blacks *must address* blacks, must *write* about blacks. Much of that early work was addressed to blacks, but it happened without my conscious intention.

When I got home I had a telegram on my dining room table from Oscar Brown, Jr., asking me to attend a preview of a musical he had developed out of the talents of the Blackstone Rangers. I went to the preview, and I was electrified. I praised the show, and asked Oscar if there were not some writers among the dancers and singers. Oscar told me there were some youngsters in the group who wanted to show me their writing. I decided to start a workshop for some of the Rangers. Haki Madhubuti (who was then Don L. Lee) came to this workshop, also Mike Cook, Johari Amini Konjufu (formerly Jewel Latimore). Walter Bradford, now a highly respected Chicago-based writer, helped me organize the Rangers. He had been working among them as a teen organizer. Walter was not a teen himself; he was in his late twenties at that time. So these "Little Rangers" would just sit there and look at me. I'll never forget that first meeting. They didn't know what in the world I was "about." And why should they? But we worked. The Rangers drifted away after awhile, but I didn't want to lose all contact with them. I asked Walter to start a Ranger workshop of his own—and I financed it. I bought books, dictionaries, various magazines for them. I paid him for a year to run the workshop, and it was quite successful.

In the meantime, a second group of young people started to meet here in my home in a workshop environment, and they were the ones who changed my whole life. They would talk about all kinds of things happening right here in Chicago. Things I knew little or nothing about: Haki introduced me to books like *The Rich and the Super Rich* [by Ferdinand Lundberg], which taught me a lot about what's going on in this society, about suppression and oppression. Haki, in fact, has had a great influence on my thinking. As a group we "workshop" people did many exciting things. We would go out and recite our poems in Malcolm X Park. In the late sixties black people put up a sign and renamed Washington park to honor Malcolm . It was *our* park, not "Washington" park. We would go to a tavern and just start reciting our poetry. Haki usually led us in, and he would say, "Look, folks, we're gonna lay some poetry on you." Then he would start reciting his poems—which were relevant. Relevant poetry was the only kind you could take into that kind of situation. Those people weren't there to listen to "Poetry," spelled with a capital P. The kind of poem I could recite in that atmosphere would be my short poem, "We Real Cool." Later on, once the atmosphere had been set by a couple of the others, who had brought tight, direct, bouncy poems, the audience would be "softened" and *ready* to listen to something of my own with more length—something like "The Life of Lincoln West."

As I said, I'm trying to create new forms, trying to do something different. I'm trying to write the kind of poem that could be presented in a tavern atmosphere—on a street corner. I always like to use the tavern as my recitation's background symbol. I also visit prisons. I go to any prison in my reciting area that invites me. The inmates are so happy to have you pay attention to them. It's really rewarding to work with them. Many inmates send me their work. And awhile back I ran a writing contest at Greenhaven Correctional Facility in Stormville, New York. It was effective. The inmates enjoyed it. *They* were the judges.

C.T.: Your earlier works, *A Street in Bronzeville* and *Annie Allen*, don't seem to focus directly on heightened political awareness. Do your more recent works tend to deal more directly with this concern?

Brooks: Well, let me just run down the table of contents of *A Street in Bronzeville* "of De Witt Williams on his way to Lincoln Cemetery," "The Sundays of Satin-Legs Smith". . . .

Many of the poems, in my new and old books, are "politically aware"; I suggest you reread them. You know, when you say "political," you really have to be exhaustive. You aren't always to think of Andy Young and his comments on Africa, for example. I try to picture in "The Sundays of Satin-Legs Smith" a young man who didn't even know he was a tool of the establishment, who didn't know his life was being run for him from birth straight to death, and even before birth. As I say in that poem: "Here are hats / Like bright umbrellas; and hysterical ties / Like narrow banners for some gathering war." Now this book was published in '45 and even then I could sense, although not brilliantly, not in great detail, that what was happening to us was going to make us erupt at some later time.

C.T.: I'm thinking of the blatant, assertive, militant posture we find in the "new black poetry" of the early seventies. Do any of your early works assume this posture, this tone?

Brooks: Yes, ma'am. I'm fighting for myself a little bit here, but not overly so, because I certainly wrote no poem that sounds like Haki's "Don't Cry, Scream" or anything like Nikki's "The True Import of Present Dialogue, Black v. Negro," which begins: "Nigger / Can you kill / Can you kill?" But I'm fighting for myself a little bit here because I believe it takes a little patience to sit down and find out that in 1945 I was saying what many of the young folks said in the sixties. But it's crowded back into language like this: "The pasts of his ancestors lean against. . . ." Or a little earlier in the same poem: "Since a man must bring / To music. . . ." In *Annie Allen* I wrote: "Let us combine. . . ." Granted, that kind of verse is not what you'd take into a tavern.

The poets of the sixties were direct. There's no doubt about it. I am the champion of those poems. I take them with me; I read them right along with my own poetry.

My works express rage and focus on *rage*. That would be true of a poem like "Negro Hero" [*A Street in Bronzeville*] and "A Bronzeville Mother Loiters in Mississippi, Meanwhile a Mississippi Mother Burns Bacon." The latter poem is from *The Bean Eaters*, which was published in '60. That book was a turning point, "politically," if you want to use that much-maligned word. So much so, in fact, that *The Bean Eaters* had a hard time getting reviewed. When it was reviewed, it got one excellent review from Robert Glauber, who used to be an editor of the *Beloit Poetry Journal*. But Frederick Bock, who was a reviewer for *Poetry* magazine, gave us to understand that he was very upset by what he thought was a revolutionary tendency in my work. I don't even remember if he used the word "revolutionary" because after all, it was 1960. He did say he thought I was bitter. He didn't like "Bronzeville Mother," or "The Lovers of the Poor." In fact, a lot of suburban white women hate "The Lovers of the Poor" to this day.

A lot of women are now observing that a good many of my poems are about women. I don't know whether you want to include woman rage in this discussion or not. But I hope you sense some real rage in "The Ballad of Pearl May Lee" [*A Street in Bronzeville*]. The speaker is a very enraged person. I know because I consulted myself on how I have felt. For instance, why in the world has it been that our men have preferred either white or that pigmentation which is as close to white as possible? That's *all* political.

C.T.: Does your post-1967 poetry suggest a black standard of beauty?

Brooks: Do you remember "at the hairdresser's" from *A Street in Bronzeville*? Well, I read it along with a recent poem called "To Those of My Sisters Who Kept Their Naturals"—with the subtitle "Never to Look a Hot Comb in the Teeth"—which is in *Primer for Blacks*. This is what I'm fighting for now in my work, for an *expression* relevant to all manner of blacks, poems I could take into a tavern, into the street, into the halls of a housing project. I don't want to say these poems have to be simple, but I want to *clarify* my language. I want these poems to be free. I want them to be direct without sacrificing the kinds of music, the picturemaking I've always been interested in. I'm not afraid of having a few remaining subtleties.

C.T.: Is there a liability in promoting the practice of segregated literary criticism? Should black writers heed criticism by black critics only?

Brooks: How are you going to force white critics to learn enough about us? Most of them have *no* interest in us or in our work. So how are you going to make them sensitive?

C.T.: I agree. But were these critics interested in any way in the works of white women before they were forced to clean up their sexist responses?

Brooks: I don't think white male critics have a great deal of interest in white women writers either. I believe whites are going to say what they choose to say about us, whether it's right or wrong, or just say *nothing*, which is another very effective way of dealing with us, so far as they are concerned. We should ignore them. I can no longer decree that we must send our books to black publishers; I would like to say that. I have no intention of ever giving my books to another white publisher. But I do know black publishers are having a lot of trouble. Many of them have disappeared from the scene. So I feel a little uneasy about saying to somebody, "Don't send your work to anyone but a black publisher." What are you going to do, send everything to Third World Press? I do believe we blacks should create more black publishing companies.

We must place an emphasis on ourselves and publish as best we can and not allow white critics to influence what we do. And if you think this is an idle statement, I know of black writers who are writing in such a way—*they think*—as to be "accepted" by the white literary world "runners." They twist their language and put in a few big-sounding words here and there, and try to obscure their meaning, thinking this will make the white literary establishment love them.

C.T.: Does it work?

Brooks: It does to a certain extent. Of course, this kind of literary "hair-straightening" is always contemptuously understood.

C.T.: Let's talk a little about the "black aesthetic."

Brooks: I'm so sick and tired of hearing about the "black aesthetic." I thought that expression had been dispensed with, that it was one of our losses following the sixties. And I was glad of that loss. What does it mean to you?

C.T.: The book, *The Black Aesthetic* [by Addison Gayle, Jr.], suggests a prescribed method of writing for black authors involving positive race images and heightened political consciousness.

Brooks: But we have been talking about this all along. An announcement that we are going to deal with "the black aesthetic" seems to me to be a waste of time. I've been talking about blackness and black people all along. But if you *need* a reply to the question, you can say I do believe in blacks writing about black life. There are many aspects of black life we need to go into further. For instance, the whole church area needs more attention. I'm not just talking about sisters in their wide hats, shouting. There's a whole lot going on in the church, and somebody ought to tackle it.

C.T.: You said earlier that people are always accusing you of not being religious.

Brooks: My poem "the funeral" [*A Street in Bronzeville*] doesn't suggest everything's going to turn out all right in the end. I hope you bear how this poem cries out for our doing something about our plight *right now,* and not depending on acquiring God or whatever. My poem "the preacher" has, in fact, been accused of being sacrilegious because I suggested that God himself might be lonely and tired of looking only down instead of across or up. The popular protest is that anything God does is right! He could never be so vulnerable as to be lonely and need someone to slap Him on the shoulder, tweak His ear, or buy Him a beer. I can't think of anything I've written that speaks sweetly of religion. My mother was "religious." Both my parents believed in doing "right." My mother, who died at the age of ninety, subscribed to dignity, decency, and duty. And she brought up her two children to subscribe to those ideals. We were taught to be kind to people. The word "kind" best describes my father. He was kind, and he believed people ought to be kind to each other. His religion was kindness. My father, as an adult, did not go to church, but he was kinder than swarms of church-goers. So I grew up thinking you're supposed to be nice. You're supposed to be good. I grew up thinking you're supposed to treat people right.

C.T.: George Kent said in *Blackness and The Adventure of Western Culture* that your poetry form-conscious and intellectual that you write from the heart and personal experience. Is his assessment accurate?

Brooks: He was a great friend of mine. He was always talking to me about my use of form, and telling me that he considered my work to be intellectual. As a matter of fact, I do not. I don't want people running around saying Gwen Brooks's work is intellectual. That makes people think instantly about obscurity. It shouldn't have to mean that, but it often seems to. I do write from the heart, from personal experience and from the experiences of other people whom I have observed. Very early in life I became fascinated with the wonders language can achieve. And I began playing with words. That word-play is what I have been known for chiefly.

You know, I would like to have nothing to do with critics. I would like to forget them. I would like to forget biographers. And I did adore George Kent! But we must have our black critics because if we don't black writers will vanish.

C.T.: You've insisted you are a black poet and not a poet who just happens to be black.

Brooks: The cultural experience of being Afro-American is integrally important to my work, but I call myself an African. This identity change was probably situated, at least officially, in 1967 because before than I called myself a Negro.

C.T.: Do you think there's been a shift in focus in the recent writings by black women, a shift from confrontation with social forces to intimate male-female encounters?

Brooks: There's a lot going on in this man-woman thing that bothers me. I'm always saying, yes, black women have got some problems with black men and vice versa, but these are family matters. They must be worked out within the family. At no time must we allow whites, males or females, to convince us that we should split. I know there's a lot of splitting going on now. And I hope it's going to stop. I don't know what's going to stop it. Maybe some poets writing some good poems can help! It's another divisive tactic dragging us from each other, and it's going to lead to a lot more racial grief. The women are not going to be winners on account of leaving their black men and going to white men, to themselves, or to nobody.

C.T.: Does your work attempt to record, to put in order black female experience?

Brooks: I think so. But I don't believe in sitting down and saying, "I'm going to use this poem as a vehicle through which life can achieve some order for black women." I get an idea. I see something happening out in the street, or somebody tells me something. Or I go into my interior and pull out something and try to put it on paper. I take a lot of notes. I start revising after the first drafts. They often sound very silly as you can see if you were to look at the stages my poems go through. Perhaps after this process, the poem will turn out to be a vehicle by which means life has reached some order, or perhaps it suggests there can be an arrival at some kind or degree of order. May not. It's not mechanical.

C.T.: What about your works in progress?

Brooks: I'm writing the second volume of my autobiography, plus a book of poems. I want to read this poem; it's the title poem of *Primer for Blacks,* a recent book of mine. I write my poems on scraps of paper because I want to carry them in my address book. I'm likely to read them at a moment's notice.

Interview

Gwendolyn Brooks / 1984

From *TriQuarterly* 60 (Spring/Summer 1984), 405–10. Reprinted by permission of *TriQuarterly* and the Estate of Gwendolyn Brooks.

Question: Why are you interviewing yourself?

GB: Because I know the facts and the nuances.

Q: Describe your "background."

GB: Nothing strange. No child abuse, no prostitution, no Mafia membership. A sparkly childhood, with two fine parents and one brother, in a plain but warmly enclosing two-storey gray house (we always rented the top floor). Our house, regularly painted by my father (sometimes with the help of his friend Berry Thompson), had a back yard and a front yard, both pleasant with hedges and shrubs and trees and flowers. My father recited fascinating poetry, and sang to us jolly or haunting songs. My favorite was "Asleep in the Deep": "Many brave hearts are asleep in the deep, so beware—be-e-e-e WARE"; his voice went down sincerely, down and down and down; suddenly the living room was a theater. My mother sang, too, and played the piano almost every day. She loved music. Classical, popular, spiritual, *all* music. She wrote music; she had gone to a class to study harmony. My parents and my brother and I observed all the holidays. We made much of the Table. It entertained, variously, turkey and pumpkin pie, fruitcake and mince pie, "Easter ham," birthday-cake creations. My brother and my mother and I (not my father) enjoyed family and church picnics, went to Riverview, Sunday School, the Regal Theatre and the Metropolitan and Harmony theaters, neighborhood parties, the Field Museum. . . . Our life was family-oriented, so we did a lot of family visiting. Aunt Ella and Uncle Ernest, Aunt Gertie and Uncle Paul lived in Chicago (all near each other now, out in Lincoln Cemetery), so we saw them frequently; but there were also aunts, uncles and cousins in Milwaukee, Topeka, and Kalamazoo, so in the summer, sometimes, we would get on a train and go visit those folks. We children enjoyed those visits so—enjoyed watching, deciphering! We enjoyed our schooltimes, too. As soon as we were old enough, my mother got us library cards; and there were many books in the house, including the Harvard Classics. Our parents were intelligent and courageous; they subscribed to duty, decency, dignity, industry—*kindness.*

Q: Why is your name, almost always, followed by the phrase "Pulitzer Prize"?

GB: Because I was the first black to be given a Pulitzer of any kind. That was in 1950, for my second book of poetry, *Annie Allen.* Thirty-three years later, another black woman has received a Pulitzer, this time for a novel, *The Color Purple,* multitalented Alice Walker). Several estimable black males won the prize in those intervening years—starting with the remarkable *Ebony* photographer, Moneta Sleet Jr. (In 1971 *Ebony* sent the two of us to Montgomery, Alabama, to work up a feature on "After-the-Storm" Montgomery. We would dash into the street; I would seize and question anyone who looked storyful, while amiable Moneta photographed away. One of the most enjoyable adventures of my life; I've always thanked Senior Editor Herb Nipson for choosing me to share that trip with Moneta.)

Q: You promised a nice little Pulitzer story.

GB: Here is a nice little Pulitzer story, one of many Pulitzer stories I'll tell you later. On Pulitzer announcement day, this past spring, I heard Alice's award mentioned on radio, minutes before I was to address an audience at the University of Missouri in Kansas City. I announced this Happening—mentioning the strange thirty-three-year gap—and asked the audience to celebrate with applause. The audience applauded. And some of the audience tsk-tsked appropriately: because, you see, in those thirty-three years black women writers had not been idle. We had Paule Marshall. We had Mari Evans. We had Maragaret Walker, Toni Cade Bambara, Audre Lorde, Lucille Clifton, Toni Morrison, Ai, Dolores Kendrick, Sonia Sanchez. Many others. Talented women. Writers of poetry *and* prose, strikingly effective *and* interesting *and* English-nourishing *and* blackness-preserving. When you really think of thirty-three years stretching between myself in 1950 and Alice in 1983, you have to gasp.

Q: Talk about the late sixties.

GB: Speaking of nourishment-my nourishment of nourishments was in the years 1967 to 1972. As I've said of those years, the "new" black ideal italicized black identity, solidarity, self-possession, self-address. Furthermore, the *essential* black ideal vitally acknowledged African roots. Came Oscar Brown Jr.'s variety show, "Opportunity, Please Knock." I met many of the Blackstone Rangers comprising, chiefly, that cast. They liked me and respected me. I started a poetry workshop for interested Rangers, college students, teen organizers. Later I paid Walter Bradford, a young organizer-friend of Oscar's, to run a one-year workshop for Rangers only. It was highly successful. My original group stayed with me several years. Eventually, many of them got teaching jobs here and there, across the country.

Among them, I had two good Sons of the Revolution. That's irony. We had no revolution. We had a healthy rebellion. Those "Sons," Walter Bradford and Don L. (Haki) Lee, taught me a little of what I needed to know about The Great World around me. I found myself reading, with profit, the books Haki recommended" such books as Fanon's *The Wretched of the Earth*, Lundberg's *The Rich and the Super-Rich*, DuBois' *The Souls of Black Folk*, Zora Neale Hurston's novels. We talked, we walked, we read our work in taverns and churches and jail. I invited writers like James Baldwin and John O. Killens to my house to meet them, to exchange views with them. At such parties, and at our own regular meetings, and at our street festivals, the air was hot, heavy with logic, illogic, zeal, construction. What years those were—years of hot-breathing hope, clean planning, and sizable black cross-reference and reliance. OF COURSE I know those years couldn't and shouldn't "return"! The flaws have been witnessed and cataloged, with great energy (and inventiveness). I needn't repeat. Much is gone and forgotten, the good and the not-good. But there's something under-river; pride surviving, pride and self-respect surviving, however, wobbly or wondering.

Well, those young people adopted and instructed me. They put me on The Wall of Respect! (Forty-third and Langley.)

The theme poem of that Blacktime's essence was Haki's "New Integrationist":

> I
> seek
> integration
> of
> negroes
> with
> Black
> people

Q: Talk about the Poet Laureate Awards.

GB: When I was made Poet Laureate of Illinois, following Carl Sandburg's death, I wanted to substantiate the honor with assistance to the young.

I spend about $2,000 each spring on a competition that involves at least twenty high-school and elementary-school awards, and a ceremony—for many years now—at the University of Chicago, with presentations, recitations. The Chicago newspapers have been cooperative, giving my young poets a forum every year.

Q: Do you feel you've had your share of honors?

GB: Indeed! There's even the Gwendolyn Brooks Junior High School at 147th and Wallace (Harvey), and the Gwendolyn Brooks Cultural Center at Western Illinois University.

Q: Have you written fiction?

GB: Short stories, and novellas I am not proud of. and a novel, *Maud Martha*, published by Harper & Row. *Maud Martha* is a lovely little novel about a lovely little person, wrestling with the threads of her milieu. Of course this "lovely little person" was the essence of myself, or aspects of myself tied with as neat a ribbon as my innocence could manage. The novel is very funny, very often!—and not at all disappointing, even *though* my heroine was never raped, did not become a lady of the evening, did not enter the world of welfare mothers (I admire Diahann Carroll's underrated movie "Claudine"), did not murder the woman who stepped on her toe in the bus. I said in my autobiographical novel "an autobiographical novel is a better testament, a better thermometer, than a memoir can be. For who, in presenting a 'factual' account, is going to tell the absolute, the horrifying or exquisite, the incredible Truth?" An autobiographical novel is allowing. There's fact-meat in the soup, among the chunks of fancy: but, generally, definite identification will be difficult. . . . Much that happened to Maudie had not happened to me; and she is a nicer and a better-coordinated creature than I am. I can say that lots in the "story" was taken out of my own life and twisted, highlighted or dimmed, dressed up or down.

Q: What is a poet? What is poetry?

GB: There are hundreds of definitions. A poet is one who distils experience—strains experience. A poet looks—sees. Poets oblige themselves to see. Poetry is siren, prose is survey. I keep telling children: "Poetry comes out of life. What happened to you yesterday and last week and six years ago and ten minutes ago and what you *surmise* may happen tomorrow is poetry-in-the-rough. Strain it—distil—work the magic of carefully-chosen *words* upon it—and there's poetry."

Q: What is the meaning of T.H.E.M.?

GB: "Trying Hard To Express Myself." I organized the eighteen teenagers on my block into a forum. T.H.E.M. was their choice of a name. They met at my house, flopped on the floor when chairage was exhausted, discussed numbers of things: school, sex, drugs, politics—Africa. One of them tired of discussions on Africa this, Africa that. She judged, "We're never going there. We're going *no*where. We're folks who have nothing at all to do with Africa." So I sent her to Ghana, with another girl from our "club," and my daughter as chaperone. Couldn't have had a better chaperone! My daughter Nora Blakely writes prose and poetry, has taught in elementary school and at Roosevelt University, dances and teaches dancing, choreographs. On the way, my voyagers had a few days in London and Paris. I wanted to help extend the horizons of these young people, and they met with me for about four years. During that time I gave them scholarships, took them to black plays and movies, bought books and educational magazines for them, brought "career people" to speak to them—writers, a senator, a photographer, an editor, an actress. They were not shy in the presence of these "career people": they challenged, corrected, extended. (These youngsters were also "watchworkers," who kept a collective eye on the block and reported disturbances to the police.) Our best-enjoyed nourishment, however, was the unrestricted exhilaration of "mere" communication.

Q: On today's scene, what excites you?

GB: Michael Jackson's "Beat It," "Billie Jean," and "Thriller" videos; the special Jackson magic is going to affect several forms of art in several years to come.

Rereadings of Moffat and Painter: *Revelations—Diaries of Women*; and *I Must Hurry for the Sea Is Coming In* by Mendota and Dalrymple; Frantz Fanon's *The Wretched of the Earth*; Joan Didion's *Salvador*; Mari Evans' *I Am a Black Woman*.

Efforts anti-nuclear. (Including "The Day After.")

Harold Washington's political sophistication and clean use of the growing esteem in which he is held; Jesse Jackson's manifested possession of world-stage genius and strength; AND, the minds of young people today: bright, striving, flexible; when I say "young" people, I go right up to the age of forty-five!

My developing suspicion that The American People, although capable of considerable amounts of self-deceit, are not lemmings, after all.

Q: Give us a piece of poetry for this time.

GB: I close a poem about Mayor Washington with three hard-felt lines:

> We begin our health.
> We enter the Age of Alliance.
> This is our senior adventure.

Not to begin our health is to begin our death. I dared to name the new age. The Age of Alliance. The inferences are obvious.

And compared to our current self-saving adventure, the games and contortions of our past have been junior.

The Age of Alliance.

Our senior adventure.

A Life Distilled: An Interview with Gwendolyn Brooks

Kevin Bezner / 1986

From *Main Street Rag* 6 (Summer 2001), 45–54. Reprinted by permission of *Main Street Rag*.

Bezner: You've written so many poems. Which of your poems do you like to read?

Brooks: I almost always read the poem "The Life of Lincoln West," which is about a little boy who has African features, and African features are not considered beautiful in the West. So nobody feels that he is pretty at all and this is made plain to him.

He doesn't have a very happy childhood until something happens that makes him zero in on the fact that he is the real thing, as somebody has said of him, not meaning it as a compliment. But he takes it as a compliment. It's an identity poem. At the end he is feeling quite happy about himself, although not understanding why. I almost always read "We Real Cool," which has been published in so many textbooks, and youngsters like it.

Bezner: Do you look back at your poems and feel that they're just not you anymore?

Brooks: No, there's some of me in all of them, even the ones I wrote as a little girl, some copies of which I have.

Bezner: Some of the poems that really struck me are the "Ballad of Pearl May Lee" and "Queen of the Blues." And "The Womanhood," which is in sections, especially "The Children of the Poor" and "I love those little booths at Benvenuti's."

Brooks: "I love those little booths. I love those little booths at Benvenuti's." I'm glad to have you mention that. I was just thinking of that poem the other day. I rarely read it. There are some poems that need to stay on the page, but I do need to drag that one out.

Bezner: I think it's an important poem. It reminds me of Richard Wright's *Native Son*, when the young white girl and her Communist friend make Bigger Thomas take them to a small, black café to see how black people live.

Brooks: That used to be a very popular sport for whites, to go to black cafes and watch the natives perform. In preparation to write this poem, my husband and I went to Benvenuti's, which is no longer in existence, but used to be notorious. It was very quiet that evening and the whites didn't get a show at all. They didn't get one from my husband and myself. With my poem, I wrote down exactly what I was looking at.

Bezner: I also like the section, "Beverly Hills, Chicago."

Brooks: That comes out of my own life. My husband and I, being very poor, used to go out on Sundays driving. We always had some little piece of car. We would drive out into the suburbs and look at those beautiful houses and say one day we would have a mansion also. We'd see the people there. We had some ridiculous idea that they were some kind of super population.

Bezner: Does any of that matter to you any longer?

Brooks: Oh, of course not. As I say when I read that poem, we grew up and met some of those people later on, and we found out that they go to the bathroom and they enjoy their chocolate cake and have domestic battles just like everyone else. And also I don't want a mansion anymore. I have a little five-room cottage in Chicago. That is where I shall end my days.

Bezner: You've said that Langston Hughes inspired you. You met him later and he dedicated one of his books to you. I was wondering how he inspired you and if you could talk a little about him.

Brooks: When I first read his poetry in an anthology I found in the library, I was very happy to learn that blacks could be published. I knew that Paul Laurence Dunbar had been published, but I always thought of him as a great specialty and it wasn't likely to happen to me. But in this book I saw Hughes's poetry and James Weldon Johnson's, the Cotters's, Joseph Senior and Junior. Nobody ever mentions them anymore.

I first met Hughes through his published poetry and then he came to read at the church my mother belonged to, Metropolitan Community Church. I later joined it, too. Haven't been there in years. My mother insisted I take some of my poems and show them to him. I did, after he read. He was very kind. He just stood there and read them. He said something to the effect, "You're very talented, keep writing. Some day you'll have a book published."

Before that I had sent poems to James Weldon Johnson, and he, too, was very helpful. He sent the poems back to me with little notes in the margins.

He didn't use the word "cliché," but that's what he meant. "This doesn't work." Those two were very helpful to me.

Later on I belonged to a poetry class run by a woman who was, at that time, a reader for *Poetry*. She had Hughes come to that class and he talked to us. That was the second time I met him.

The third time I gave a party for him. It was such a lot of fun, and he thought so, too. He said it was the best party that had ever been given for him.

Later he came over to the house, just popped in one day to our little kitchenette and we had mustard greens, ham hocks, cornbread, that kind of thing. He was very down to earth, warm, friendly, very helpful to young people.

Bezner: When Hughes told you you were talented you must have felt quite good about your work.

Brooks: Oh, yes. I felt, shall I say, legitimized. Later I saw him here at the Library of Congress. They had a poetry festival here in 1962. We were all here.

There were so many poets. John Berryman, who later committed suicide. Randall Jarrell. They're still wondering whether or not he committed suicide. I'm mentioning people who are dead now.

I went down the list of the people who were here, and I found scads of them who are now dead. Oscar Williams. Louis Untermeyer, the great anthologist. I really loved his anthologies. He had a double one called Modern American and British Poetry. That was really a school for me.

Bezner: Was it really? Allen Ginsberg also said he was influenced by that anthology.

Brooks: He did? I feel good about hearing that. That's fascinating. I'm glad you told me that. I used to sit out in the park with that double anthology and wait for my son to get out of kindergarten. It was a real companion.

Bezner: Are there any poets in that anthology who had a particular influence?

Brooks: I believe it must have been there that I met Eliot. And Wallace Stevens. Of course, I had two years of junior college, and I remember having a very good literature teacher. I can't remember what we read. Emily Dickinson, Walt Whitman. It was a course in American literature.

Bezner: Your early poems seem to be influenced by Emily Dickinson.

Brooks: I loved her poetry when I was young. I still go back to it from time to time. She was a good poet. She knew how to make a little powerhouse out of a phrase. She would string common words together and make magic. I can appreciate that.

Bezner: You've said before to "keep the rhythms loose" and to "write human talk."

Brooks: And not have it like a metronome. Our poetry is richer if it is looser, takes chances.

Bezner: You seem to try to follow these suggestions.

Brooks: Not always. I've broken all my rules. And one of the things I'd like to say is that I'm still in process. I have many, many things to teach myself. I'm trying to write a different kind of poetry now, although "kind" is not the word to use. It's less rigid.

If rhyme is used it's used irregularly, or it seems to be used irregularly. I've probably scheduled it, but you're supposed to think that it's helter-skelter, harem-scarem. I'm trying to write poetry that will appeal immediately but still might be understood on several levels.

Bezner: In 1967 you attended the Fisk University Black Writers Conference, and this seemed to change your attitude toward writing.

Brooks: Before that, I, too, had liked the sound of the word "universal." And I thought in terms of reaching everyone in the world with my poetry.

But then I met some young blacks who had a different idea. They thought that black poetry was written by blacks, about blacks, to blacks. That last is often changed to "for blacks," which really throws it all off kilter as far as I'm concerned.

I think that poetry is for anybody who wants to take the time to consult it. These people felt, and the more I listened to them the more sensible it sounded, that there was a lot that blacks had to say to each other.

Bezner: In your autobiography you say that you were "respected" at the time, and it's almost as if you felt you were begrudgingly respected.

Brooks: No, that wasn't it at all. Those were times when blacks really felt themselves to be family. This was inclusive of not only people here but people across the seas in Africa, Brazil. Wherever blacks were they were supposed to consider themselves a part of this great black family. Unless you're talking about this conference still.

Bezner: Yes, the conference.

Brooks: Oh, that's entirely different. This new spirit was just beginning.

Leroi Jones was still Leroi Jones, not Immamu Amiri Baraka, as he became soon after that. I was reading there, as was Margaret Danner, another black poet. She was about four years older than I. She's dead now. We were both respected. *Respected.*

I like your putting little quotes around respected. Respected but not enjoyed as was later a poet like Nikki Giovanni. I didn't know anything about Nikki then, although she was writing.

People like the then Don Lee, Mwalimu Haki R. Madhubuti, who wasn't known then. He was standing out on street corners selling copies of his poems to passersby or reading out at the park, which later on we all did. And in taverns.

That conference was the beginning of much for me.

Bezner: In reading your early poems, such as "The Womanhood," it seems that there is a similarity between what they were trying to do and what you were doing earlier in feeling.

Brooks: Oh, thank you. I feel that way about some of the poems I had published then. And, of course, I was doing readings then and often among these young people.

Everything just blew up, you know, right after that conference. And they would have huge—talk about poetry audiences—huge, overflowing audiences composed of black people.

There were always a few whites who would come. But they were, should I call them, honorary whites, as blacks are called if they're high enough and rich enough to go to South Africa. You know that, don't you?

But anyway, these people loved poetry, but it had to be the kind of poetry that was immediately accessible, and it often had obscenities in it. It often was a little column of expletives.

There was a kind of poem that came to be known to us as a "kill the honky" poem. I doubt that you'd see any of that poetry today. I don't know anybody who's writing such poetry today.

Bezner: It sounds as if that anger was necessary.

Brooks: It was. I felt it was. It was rather cleansing. I would read some of my poetry and they would like one that you mentioned, "The Ballad of Pearl May Lee," and "We Real Cool." And after I had written it, they liked "Riot." But that wasn't written until after Martin Luther King was killed.

Bezner: How did you feel when you won the Pulitzer Prize in 1950? You were the first black to win the prize. It must have been startling.

Brooks: Yes, it was startling to a lot of people. And certainly to me. You have probably heard this story, but I'll repeat it for you.

I received this news in the dark because our lights had been turned off. We were poor and sometimes we lost our electricity. On this occasion I was sitting in the dark with my little son.

The telephone rang and Jack Star, who was on the staff of the Chicago *Sun-Times*, said, "Do you know that you have won the Pulitzer Prize for poetry?" And I screamed and said I didn't believe it.

So my son and I celebrated by going to the movies after dancing around the room.

Bezner: Do you remember what you saw?

Brooks: People always ask me that. I don't, and I can't understand why.

Bezner: You probably didn't think it was important.

Brooks: It should have been. The next day the photographers came, reporters came. I was scared stiff about the electricity. I didn't say one word. You would have thought I'd say, "Well, there's no point to putting the plug in because there's no electricity." I just sat there and watched them put the plugs in, and lo, there was light.

I have never known what happened. I don't know if my husband scurried around and got them turned on, or maybe the city turned them on.

Bezner: How did the black community react?

Brooks: Everybody was very happy about it. See, this had never happened to a black before.

Bezner: There seems to be a real concern for place and the people of those places in your work. Chicago, for instance.

Brooks: I can perhaps help by saying how *A Street in Bronzeville* was written. I was raised on a street in Chicago called Champlain Avenue, 43rd and Champlain Avenue.

I lived in a house there which was burned down a couple of years ago. That's where I was raised. I responded to that street. I grew up there. I got married from that house at the age of twenty-two.

I decided that I was going to write this book called *A Street in Bronzeville*. I went up and down the street and made notes of houses that had seen something exciting happen. For instance, there's a poem in there called "The Murder." A little boy lived next door with his little baby brother and had set his baby dress on fire. Accidentally, of course. The baby died. After that, the one remaining kept on asking the neighbors, "When is Percy coming back?"

That wasn't the boy's name, but I gave him that name. So I picked out something that really happened in those houses or a special personality like the one in "the vacant lot." There was a young woman who became a very good friend of mine. She was there after she had married the boy I had grown up with, Robert, his name was. She got pregnant, and in those days folks had to marry.

He married her, but unwillingly, because his mother made him. So that gave me two poems, "the vacant lot" and "when Mrs. Martin's Booker T." [She picks up the book *The World of Gwendolyn Brooks* and reads the poem. In the poem, Booker T. impregnates Rosa Brown. Because she feels disgraced by her son, Mrs. Martin moves to another side of town. She wants no news of her son, unless it is the news that he has married Rosa.]

Well, now, that's really the way the woman felt, although she didn't look like that poem sounds. She was very elegant, very dark. She really believed in a man taking care of his responsibilities. Who knows that she might have, with that beautiful moral attitude, wrecked those two lives. That young man was absolutely miserable. They both lived perfectly wretched lives.

But I'm reading that poem to you for another reason. Never again will I write a poem that sounds like that, that just ripples on, is easily rhymed, and just spills out of the consciousness.

Bezner: But you're still able to read that poem powerfully.

Brooks: I'm not saying I'm sorry I wrote it. I'm just saying it will never be written again.

Bezner: Do you still have sources for your poems as you did with your earlier poems? You said you write notes every day. Do you observe what is happening around you?

Brooks: Oh yes, and I'm inspired by what I see on TV. The latest poem I've written is called "The Near-Johannesburg Boy." Meaning he doesn't live in Johannesburg. He lives in Soweto.

I wrote that poem because I had been seeing these terrible pictures on TV of what is happening in South Africa. And what specifically inspired the poem is what I heard the children were saying to each other: "Have you been detained yet?" I heard that reported. They were just so used to being piled into jail that it was just like having a barbecue here. It was an experience that you just went through.

Bezner: Are you writing a lot of political poems these days?

Brooks: I don't call anything I write political, but I'm moved by what is happening in the world just as anybody else would be. I use the word "barbecue" a lot. If I went to a barbecue in somebody's back yard—which, incidentally, is an activity I absolutely loathe—if something exciting happened there I would report it.

I often think of myself as a reporter. When I was not as modest as I am now I think I would refer to myself as the super reporter. I don't call that being political, I just call that human and responding to what you see and feel around you.

Bezner: Why not political?

Brooks: I think that word has been abused, and often it is used to scold someone. You might be told that you are a political poet as a kind of castigation. It's an accusation.

Bezner: That those who write political poems cannot do universal poems?

Brooks: I don't think that's what they have in mind at all when they are scolding you. People who accuse you of writing political poetry mean that you're almost a Communist.

Bezner: James Merrill is somewhat disdainful of political poetry and has said that when you deal with political subjects in poems you have to be careful.

Brooks: When people see what you're about they, I don't want to say all people, that's not true at all, we're talking about a certain breed. But for heaven's sake, if children are being shot, people are being burned, and all those other things that are happening in South Africa, and you talk about them, why would your poem be called political? That is something that is happening in the world. I always say that poetry is life distilled.

A Conversation with Gwendolyn Brooks

Alan Jabbour and Ethelbert Miller / 1986

Conducted and videotaped at the Library of Congress. Reprinted by permission of Alan Jabbour, Ethelbert Miller, and the Library of Congress.

Jabbour: We're here today for a conversation with Gwendolyn Brooks. Ms. Brooks is just completing her term as the 29th Consultant in Poetry for the Library of Congress. She has a distinguished career as a poet, having been named as a recipient of the Pulitzer Prize and she's the Poet Laureate of the State of Illinois and many other honors have come her way. It's an honor for us to have her here today to talk with her. With me is Ethelbert Miller, who is a poet himself and director of the Afro-American Resource Center at Howard University, and, I might add, a long-time fan of Gwendolyn Brooks.

Ms. Brooks, your visit here at the Library of Congress has stirred up all sorts of excitement with people here. I'll have to report this to you as a staff member of the Library. Everybody has been tremendously enthusiastic about the way you've thrown yourself into the task of being consultant in poetry and particularly I keep hearing stories about how you always find time to talk to anybody who comes and to write them letters. Even with children or perhaps especially with children you seem to take time out to work with them. Have you always been that way with children?

Brooks: Yes, I do enjoy working with children and talking with them. They're amazing. I had about thirty children in this very poetry room about a week ago and what a time we had. They talked about not just poetry, but about their grandmothers, about beer, about pizza, and about hair. (laughter) When I came here I thought that's what I was supposed to do. To share my feelings about poetry with anyone who was interested.

Miller: You have the honor of winning the Pulitzer, and you won it I think when you were thirty-three, which I guess as a writer would be very young for winning that type of award. Was there any sort of jealously from some of your peers because all of a sudden you win the Pulitzer Prize at thirty-three?

Brooks: Thirty-two. (laughter) If there was, they didn't tell me. And I was

too excited and happy to be looking for any such evidences. My friends were
seemingly very proud and happy. It was something that hadn't happened to
a Black before so they were glad on that score. We had a lot of celebrations
I remember.

Miller: How did you hear about it? Because there's always the thing of
the person being notified. How did you hear about it? Where were you when
you heard that you had won the Pulitzer Prize?

Brooks: I was in a house at 9134 Wentworth and the lights were out.
That's been told many times by now. We hadn't paid the electric bill so there
was no electricity. It was dusk, so it was dark in the house. My son was nine
at the time. Jack Starr, a reporter on the *Sun Times* called. He is now associated with *Chicago Magazine*, was one of the editors, senior editor until just
recently. So he said, "Do you know that you have won the Pulitzer Prize?"
And I said "no" and screamed over the telephone. I couldn't believe it. So
he said well it was true and it would be announced the next day. The next
day reporters came, photographers came with cameras and I was absolutely
petrified. I wasn't going to say anything about the electricity. I knew that
when they tried to attach their cameras and all, nothing was going to happen.
However, miraculously, somebody had turned the electricity back on that
fast. I've never known exactly what happened. So my son and I danced
around in the dusk and decided we'd go out to the movies to celebrate. I
don't know what movie it was before you ask. (laughter)

Miller: Ms. Brooks, one person whom I had an opportunity to talk to
while you were here at the Library of Congress was your daughter Nora, and
one thing I was struck by was the closeness between you and her. It seemed
more like sisters as opposed to mother-daughter. And I know she has been
the inspiration to some of your work, which you have dedicated to her. Could
you talk about that relationship?

Brooks: Sisters? I think she always remembers that I'm mother and I
remember that she's daughter because I'm still likely to adjust the collar or
something and irritate her in that way. But we are good friends and we see
many things alike. For instance, when she went to Paris, she went to France
when she was about fifteen and she came back with a natural. She had gone
there with her hair all nicely curled and oiled and shinning and I expected
her to come back that way. She came back with a natural and we had it hot
and heavy then, believe it or not. But she stood by her decision and that is
something I've always admired in her. She has helped me many times just as

have so many of those young people that I met in the 60s. I've learned a lot from the young.

Miller: You went on to write a poem about the natural. Is this part of that?

Brooks: Later on. Much later on when I had a natural. "To those of my sisters who kept their naturals." Under which I say never to look a hot comb in the teeth. It has irritated a lot of my sisters.

Miller: You've mentioned a lot about Haki Madhubuti and at some time he seems to have been your mentor to Black consciousness. Sometimes he seems to have been your son in terms of a person who . . .

Brooks: Yes, you know the situation exactly.

Miller: There seems to be a suitable amount of warmth between you and him, and I was wondering if you could talk a little about his career.

Brooks: Well, I do think of him as a son. I met him in 1967. He came to join that little workshop I had for the Black Stone Rangers. Very soon that became a workshop chiefly devoted to teenagers, college students and teenage organizers. Haki was a college student at that time. I very soon found out that there was much quality there, much adventurousness in the writing because I understand that he was influencing even people like the Last Poets. You remember the Last Poets? I've heard that they were much inspired by his daring do. He was always very kind to me. He and Walter Bradford, another poet in Chicago, sort of adopted me at that very sensitive time.

Miller: What do you mean "sensitive time"?

Brooks: Well, there was revolt all around us especially when Martin Luther King, Jr. was killed, but even before that, there was an understanding that Blacks were to think better of themselves, to have more of a respect for themselves, to care for themselves, and to certainly learn much about their heritage that they, many scores of them, did not know. So Haki and Walter introduced me to books that I'd never heard of. They were responsible for me reading the *Autobiography of Malcolm X, The Rich and the Super Rich*, by Ferdinand Lundberg. That book taught me a lot about what was going on in our society. And I had been this little Alice in Wonderland drifting. I mean I had certain strong feelings, as you can tell when you read some of the poems in my first book, *A Street in Bronzeville*, but I hadn't organized my feelings and they helped me.

Miller: You had a number of people in your series, whom I know many people in Washington were pleased to see. One person was James Baldwin, who came and read, and he's been very distinguished. When did you meet him?

Brooks: In 1968, I believe it was. He came over to my house at my invitation to talk with some of those riotous young people that I was associated with at that time. Most of them poets and essayists, and he came and curled up on my sofa, as you know because you know him. He is one of the warmest hearted people that you could possibly meet in spite of his having written *The Fire Next Time*! He was very forthcoming with these young folks. He let them question him and harangue him. I remember Haki got disgusted with something that he had said one point and said, "Man have you ever heard of napalm?" and he wasn't being sweet to James Baldwin at all, but he rather enjoyed it and took it all in stride.

Jabbour: People talk about poets influencing other poets, but I suppose there are different kinds of influence. Perhaps there is poetic or career influence, but also perhaps spiritual influence. What kind of influences did you receive from those that came before you?

Brooks: There is the famous story, famous with me anyway, about my meeting with James Weldon Johnson when I was sixteen years old. My mother had insisted that we go to hear him lecture at a church, and after the lecture she insisted that we go up and talk with him. I was scared to death, much as Ethelbert reports with his cohorts, models. I said, "How do you do?" And my mother said, "This is Gwendolyn Brooks, she is the one who wrote you all those letters." (laughter) So he said, "I get so many of them you know." (laughter) Which was perfectly reasonable, but of course it kind of chilled us a bit. Shortly after that, we went to another church, our own church, Metropolitan Community Center in Chicago, to hear Langston Hughes, and he was entirely different. This time, my mother had armed me with manuscripts, and she insisted that I take these to Langston, and he stood right there and read them and said something like, "You're talented, keep writing. Someday you'll have a book published." That did mean a lot to a sixteen year-old girl.

Jabbour: I dare say you provide the same sort of moral or spiritual inspiration to other younger poets. You may not have personally made their career, but maybe you were there at that magic moment.

Brooks: Well, you never know what is the magic moment so I am encouraging to anyone who is writing with seriousness. I'm a little discouraged with children, teenagers, even adults, will say, "Where can I get my poetry published or how much money can I make"? It's saddening to me, but I give them practical aides. I ask them to read a lot of poetry, to write a lot, to keep a journal. Some of them are frightened by that word journal, so I say keep a notebook in which you have your thoughts, your feelings, your worries, your angers.

Jabbour: Do you feel that it's a burden or responsibility at this stage in your career to speak to other poets or to speak for the Black community or for Chicagoans or anything like that? I was thinking of the Pulitzer, and I was wondering to what degree these awards create a feeling of responsibility to others.

Brooks: No, they have not made me aware of a sense of responsibility. I do feel responsible as anyone with any decency would feel, but I must hop right in here and tell you I do not speak for "the Black community." There are many aspects to that community and I just talk about how I feel. Many of my brother and sisters feel the same way, but then there are others who do not. For instance, I went to Wellesley, I needn't specify that college, but this event was situated there. It could have been any other college and it has been since then. But some years ago, about three years ago, I read there and during a questions-and-answers period, a young Black woman asked me, "Why do you keep talking about blackness? We all know that the time for that is over. We are now merely Americans." And she said she was, for her part, tired of hearing about blackness. I consider this as very alarming and I point out when I mention this that the Jews for all the problems that they might have with themselves, still manage to come together to work toward importances. They are not ashamed of their heritage. The Chinese are proud to be Chinese. The Japanese are proud to be Japanese and I'd like for Blacks to be proud of what they have come from. They've got a lot to be proud of. First of all, they need to learn that and find out that they do have much to be proud of. So I would not be speaking for her, (laughter) my little questioner.

Miller: But it's interesting in terms of when you deal with the Black community and you won an award, let's say for example the Pulitzer, all of a sudden you're elevated, you're the first to win this award and you look up and people see you as being a spokesperson. You've been a person who has received a number of honorary degrees, so I guess with that achievement comes that type of responsibility. Would you agree or disagree?

Brooks: I would say that Blacks should get busy and create some awards of their own. We need to have one of our wealthy Black men or women create awards to the tune of say $100,000. If there were a prize with that amount attached to it, I think that there would be a lot of respect that we don't have now.

Miller: There's one poem, you know, many times writers are thought of in terms of one poem. Sometimes people think of Langston Hughes's "I've Known Rivers" and it seems as if when people think of Gwendolyn Brooks sometimes they think of "We Real Cool." I think that's a poem that's been anthologized quite a bit. How do you feel about that poem?

Brooks: It's the only poem that I've written that sounds exactly like that, but it has been published in a lot of anthologies and school textbooks. Children like it, young people like it, because it has a kind of insouciance and a staccato effect that they enjoy. And I was really gratified when I read it and talked about poetry at the Howard Woodson High School in Washington here. Young people, boys that first time, because I've gone back and they've done it again with girls in the mixture, jumped up from all over the large room, the library chanting that poem, snapping their fingers rhythmically. I love that. If you want to have a little background on the poem, I wrote it because I was passing by a pool hall in my neighborhood in Chicago one afternoon and I saw, well as I said in the poem, seven boys shooting pool and I wondered how they felt about themselves. And I decided that they felt they were not quite valid and that they certainly were insecure. They were not quite cherished by the society. Therefore they would feel that they should spit in the face of the establishment. I use the month of June as an establishment symbol. Whereas the rest of us love and respect June and wait for it to come so we can enjoy it, they would *jazz June* as I said before, derange in it and scratch in it and do anything that would annoy the establishment.

Jabbour: Could I get you to recite that poem? I'd love to hear the way you read it and accent it.

Gwendolyn Brooks reads, "We Real Cool."

Miller: Ms. Brooks, I want to get your assessment of many of the women writers that have emerged in the last fifteen years and I want you to talk about that in relationship to people like Margaret Danner and May Miller, Margaret Walker, some of the earlier Black women writers and what they were focusing on and what many recent Black women writers have been writing about.

Brooks: I think all of them had many ideas and convictions in common.

They were all concerned about race matters. Margaret Walker perhaps most socially oriented. And you wanted me to mention people of today?

Miller: Mention something about Margaret Danner, because people forget about her.

Brooks: Yes, Margaret Danner. Did you happen to know her?

Miller: I met her maybe twice.

Brooks: She and I were very close friends in the forties, just before my first book was published, which was in 1945. We had long conversations about poetic technique. We would read lots and lots of poetry and talk about it most seriously. Margaret belonged with me to a little group that was called the Poetry Class. It was organized by Inez Cunningham Stark, she was then. She later moved to Washington and married an ornithologist named Regerick Bolton. But back in Chicago, she started this class for young Blacks on the South Side and to it came Margaret Danner and she was at that time very inexperienced in writing poetry. She hadn't been writing very long, I believe. Her work had a lot of clichés in it. She was our great success story because she became the most technically astute of all that group of say maybe about twelve people. I don't believe she ever did get her due in attention.

Miller: In looking at her and yourself and looking at say the Alice Walkers and the Ntozake Shanges, do you see their careers as being different or their work being different?

Brooks: Yes, their careers are sassier and they are very interested in manner, more so I believe than the ones that you just asked me about were back in the forties. I'm very proud of what they're able to do with language and they're admired everywhere I go.

Miller: Has Gwendolyn Brooks been influenced by the women's movement in this country?

Brooks: I'm very glad that women are speaking out for themselves. I felt that there was a danger there for Black women in earlier times. I hope that that time is over. I would often take part in panel discussions with some of the, as they were called then, women's libbers; not great people like Gloria Steinem or Betty Friedan, but others who were quite hot on the subject. They, many of them, hated, hated, hated men. Hated their own men, hated any men, and I felt that that was a trap that Black women must not fall into because we are lost without the understanding that if we don't pull together, well, we won't be here to pull at all.

Miller: You have a term, which I thought was so funny, "literary hair straightening." You've used this expression.

Brooks: Have I?

Miller: Right. It's in an interview you did with Claudia Tate, in her book, *Black Women Writers at Work*, and you talk about the whole thing of writers, Black writers, almost removing the blackness in their work to make it fit more in terms of white literature. I was wondering about the future of Black writers, which way do they go in terms of being successful in communicating with their audience.

Brooks: Well, that in itself was a bounce back to, say, the forties and the early fifties, so I would hope that we could avoid zeroing in on our past and would really see that there is some richness to be dealt with. There are many, many stories that need to be told about Blacks; real love stories involving all ages. There is a wonderful script that is to be aired in the fall. The dialogue was written by William Branch; he teaches at Cornell and I got to see there this half-hour show called *A Letter from Booker T.* The stars are Ruby Dee and Ossie Davis and it is one of the most sensitive and nuanceful pieces I have ever seen. It has humor, that one of you mentioned. Humor is important because it is part of life. It has wit, mischief, and love. All of these items are part of Black life and I would like to see them stressed in our art.

Interviews with Gwendolyn Brooks

Rebekah Presson / 1988

Broadcast on "New Letters on the Air" November 1988. Interview originally conducted in April 1988. Reprinted by permission of *New Letters* and the Curators of the University of Missouri/Kansas City.

Brooks: I've written so many poems that I believe some of them will stay alive. People write me wonderful letters saying that this poem or that poem has meant very much to them and in some cases has changed their direction, so I hope I'll still be useful when I'm no longer here.

Presson: Which poem gets the most votes from people who write and talk to you?

B: Well I'd have to say that "We Real Cool" is probably the most popular poem I've written. But another poem that I'll read tonight is "The Life of Lincoln West," about a little boy who has a hard time because he is not judged beautiful by his society. This is because he looks African.

P: I think you read that the last time I saw you read. Is it "God Don't Like Ugly?"

B: I read it almost all the time and cringe when people say, "Read that poem about that little ugly boy," because the whole idea is, he's not ugly. He is insulted! He's African looking, which is wonderful.

P: That's the problem with a poem isn't it? Once you let go of it, you have no control on how people interpret it.

B: Isn't that true? And of course that's one of the richnesses of poetry, that each one of us gives something to a poem. Hopefully, you'll get something that the poet put there for you. But because you are you, unique, different from everybody else, and have had different experiences, you're going to give something to that poem. Make it richer for your own use.

P: Would you mind reading "We Real Cool"?

Brooks reads "We Real Cool."

B: And of course that death doesn't have to be a physical death, though it very often is. It could be, however, a mental or a moral or a spiritual death.

P: That poem is almost a precursor of rap, isn't it?

B: I wonder what the rapsters would say about that, but thank you. I don't think so. I really believe that's something entirely different.

P: Maybe it's just the way you recite it. You know, the way you hit the line endings that way so that it almost sounds like it could be rap.

B: Your listeners might be interested in knowing why I put a "we" at the end of each line until you get to the last line. First, when I first wrote the poem, oh, so many years ago, I said, "We real cool / we left school / we learned late." But then it occurred to me that these are youngsters; that's why I wrote the poem really. These are youngsters who don't have much attention. They would like some attention. They'd like to be looked at with some respect and affection by their society. So I decided to put the "we" at the end so that you would have to pause just a split second and give them just a split second's worth of attention.

P: What a wonderful idea. Now "We Real Cool" comes from your third book, *The Bean Eaters*. You won the Pulitzer Prize for your second book.

B: *Annie Allen*. *The Bean Eaters* is a much better book.

P: That was my question.

B: And so is *In the Mecca*. And perhaps, *A Street in Bronzeville*, the very first. But you never know with judges.

P: That's not the way it happened.

B: Judges are interesting. I have been a judge. I was a judge for the Pulitzer once and a judge for the National Book Award twice, and I can tell you some exciting things go on in those judging rooms. And the upshot of it all is that judges are human beings and they do things for a variety of reasons.

P: Are they honest reasons?

B: I believe that they all want to be honest.

P: You don't want to comment further on that, do you?

B: Welllll. Welllll!

P: A lot of politics gets involved in spite of it all?

B: As I pointed out, they are human.

P: Okay. In your first book, in fact, I hope you will read this poem, in *A Street in Bronzeville*, you write about abortion in a way that is so bright and truthful that it's frightening to read, even in 1988. I wonder how a voice like yours managed to be heard in 1945 on a subject like that. What did people say when they read, "A Mother"?

B: Well, people are still saying, sometimes, that they'd prefer I'd not include that poem in a program.

P: Would you like to include it in our program?
B: I've already read it on your campus. And I'll read it again if you. . . .

P: I'd love you. . . .
B: Oh, you mean right here and now?

P: Right here. Yes.
B: Surely, if you want me to. It's right here.

P: Because that's such a stunningly modern poem, I just can hardly believe that it was written in 1945.

B: Interesting. Well, first I'll tell you that I wrote it because I had a friend who had had several abortions. And she told me how she felt about her experience. And that is what I put into this poem. As I told Dan Jaffey's class this afternoon, I understand that not every woman feels the same about that kind of encounter.

Brooks reads "The Mother."

P: That's very sad.

B: It has a kind of joy and life, though. And I feel that it shouldn't be called "an abortion poem" as it so often is called. I have a little catalog here of the qualities of motherhood, which I hope are not customarily missed.

P: "The sucking thumb."
B: Yes. Or "scuttle" . . . and you will "never wind up the sucking thumb."

P: And the feeding. . . .
B: Or "scuttle off ghosts that come." You will never leave them, controlling your luscious sigh," that is glad to get away from them for a while, but "return for a snack of them with gobbling mother-eye," which is an aspect of motherhood that I think is familiar to most mothers.

P: Going and looking in the cradle at night? Is that what that is?
B: No. Getting out of the house, away from those children you love so much and going downtown and looking in the shop windows or shopping. Going for lunch with a friend. Whatever you like to do, doing it. But at a

certain time in that experience, you want to get back to those kids. You can hardly wait to get back and see their dear little faces. Well, this poem is called "The Mother," so I'd like all the aspects of motherhood to be considered.

P: Okay.

This is New Letters on the Air and my guest is the Pulitzer Prize winning poet who is also the poet/laureate of Illinois, Gwendolyn Brooks.

P: Now, you've really stayed in Chicago all your life, but you were nonetheless affiliated with some of the major members of the Harlem Renaissance and they . . .

B: Really?

P: Well, is that not true?

B: Only one. Langston Hughes.

P: That's pretty important. What I was wondering is, how the different movements in poetry have affected your life and your poetry. I know that's an awfully big question, but maybe you could sort of glance over how you were affected first by the Renaissance and then by the Black Liberation Movement of the late 60s.

B: Well I was certainly affected by Langston Hughes. But my introduction to the Harlem Renaissance, I didn't even think about it in such terms until I was grown and kept hearing other people talk about it, because that is a subject that teacher's love to deal with. Love to talk about. The Harlem Renaissance. But I wrote to James Weldon Johnson, author of *God's Trombones*, you know, which includes that beautiful poem, "Creation." Almost everybody who loves literature does know that poem and the Negro National Anthem. And I wish that name could be changed. I'll bet if he were alive, he would change it.

P: To what?

B: But then I haven't changed the name of a poem that one of your friends likes, "The Negro Hero," to "The Black Hero."

Well, let's see. James Weldon Johnson wrote back to me and criticized the poems that I had sent him. His way of criticizing was to write in the margins what he thought of this or that. How this could be improved. He didn't use the word ever, that I remember, but that's what he meant. And he didn't like my reversing certain words, which is an old poet's trick—an old, old, old, old trick of poets such as Wordsworth, Keats, Shelley. So he said I ought to read more modern poets. Not to imitate them, but just to know what was being done today. That led me to read people like um, . . .

P: T. S. Eliot?

B: Yes, T. S. Eliot and e. e. cummings, other people like that. And I went to the library and discovered . . . it was just about this time that I discovered a little book called *Caroling Dusk*, which contained poems by Harlem Renaissance-ers. And I became acquainted with Countee Cullen and Claude McKay and Sterling Brown and the two Cotters and Fenton Johnson, who wrote that fascinating poem, "Tired": "I shall go down to the Last Chance Saloon. . . ."

So, that was my invitation. Langston Hughes I met because he was coming to recite at the church my family went to. I say my family, but my father never went to church in all the time I knew him. But he had grown up in the church. And I think he was glad to have a little rest of it. But he was the kindest soul I have ever met. I had wonderful parents.

My mother insisted that I show my poems to Langston Hughes. He stood there and read some of them and said, "You're very talented. Keep writing. Someday you'll have a book published."

So he was very proud. I knew him after I got married. Gave a party for him once. Seventy-five people in a one-room kitchenette at 623 E. 63rd St., Chicago. I just passed by that place yesterday. It's still there. But the neighborhood has greatly changed.

P: For the worse or the better?

B: Oh, for the worse.

P: So, then, did he keep criticizing your work?

B: No, that was all. There was no more criticism, just appreciation.

P: Just a word of encouragement. Okay. All right. So you were writing pretty much formal structured poems?

B: Yes.

P: All along, until the late '60s right?

B: Oh no, I did write many poems in free verse. And many in iambic pentameter. "The Sundays of Satin Legs Smith" is essentially iambic pentameter.

P: In your early work you depend pretty heavily on rhyme and on meter in the formal elements of poetry but you did write some free verse. But now

I read in the late 1960s you had an epiphany upon hearing Amiri Baraka speak. Is that true? What happened there?

B: It wasn't Amiri Baraka speaking, although he did come to that conference that you're referring to. It was at Fisk University in '67 and I had gone out there to give a reading and Margaret Cunningham was giving a reading. She later became Margaret Danner, and she's dead now, and I noticed something different about this conference. There were young poets running around showing their poems to each other and to me, too. One of them was Ron Milner, who became a very famous playwright. And these people seemed to have a different idea about what they should be doing, poetry-wise. And they had a motto, an essential motto: "Black Poetry is poetry written by blacks, about blacks, to blacks." It is very important to say, "to." It has been translated often into "for," which just throws everything out of kilter, because at that time they were interested chiefly in a black audience. They were interested in a black audience. Still in all, I feel, and many of them felt and feel now, and have felt long since, that poetry is for anybody who wants to pick it up and subscribe to it.

But what they really wanted to do was to address themselves to blacks because they had so much to say to blacks. For instance, I'll give you an example of the kind of thing that if I had written in at that time I would have felt would be a good illustration. It is anyway. I have a poem called, "To Those of My Sisters Who Kept Their Naturals," and underneath that interesting title I have the little legend: "Never to look a hot-comb in the teeth."

Well now, there is no need in my addressing that poem to whites because they are very happy with what they have on top of their heads. But not all of my sisters are. So, would you like me to read that poem?

P: Oh yes, very much.

Brooks reads "To Those of My Sisters"

B: I get some mean looks sometimes when I read that poem.

P: Do you think that is what your poetry is about, though? Teaching self-love, self-acceptance?

B: Well, I certainly wouldn't make that kind of announcement. My poetry is here to teach self-reliance and self-acceptance. I have poems about flowers. And of course I went to this conference, which you call an epiphany, in '67. I started writing when I was seven, printing when I was eleven when I sent four poems to a Chicago paper and they published them. They didn't know I was eleven, so they published all four of them. That really set me up.

But a poem like "The Life of Lincoln West," of course, I frankly call an identity poem. Though I didn't sit down and say, "I am now going to write an identity poem," I wrote about a situation that is very, very familiar to blacks. All blacks. The poem begins: "Ugliest little boy that everyone ever saw / That was what everyone said."

So all blacks know exactly what I am talking about. And at the end when this little boy is able to say, after hearing someone else say it who had no intention of praising him, "I am the realllllll thing!" I hope people will pick up on that and understand just what I mean. And as I say, blacks certainly will.

Little Caucasian ladies, however, have said to me, "Oh, I just love that poem because I had a sister and she was prettier than I, and I know just how Lincoln West felt."

P: And are they right?

B: Well, I mean, it's what I say, that poetry, you know, you take what you need from it.

A Conversation with Gwendolyn Brooks

Susan Elizabeth Howe and Jay Fox / 1990

From *Literature and Belief* 12 (1992), 1–12. Reprinted by permission of Susan Elizabeth Howe and Jay Fox and *Literature and Belief*.

The following are responses to questions posed to Gwendolyn Brooks by Susan Elizabeth Howe, Jay Fox, and students in a contemporary American poetry class at Brigham Young University on 27 November 1990.

Question: When I read your poetry, what do you hope that I will see?

Brooks: Earlier you mentioned a poem called "A Song in the Front Yard." I think that poem just says what it wants to say and is not at all difficult to understand. You don't need to come upon it sneakily. It says that a little girl wants to be as free as her friends. She doesn't want to stay behind the front gate at a quarter to nine. She wants to be free to go and mingle with her friends and even go back to the alley and play if she wants to. Along with a lot of other blacks, I really began to hate the word *universal* because when it was used it often excluded the experience of blacks. But certainly if anything is universal, it is a child's wish not to be constrained.

Q: So it is not that we cannot learn something from your poems about what it is like to be a black woman, we just can't tell exactly what a particular person is representing in a particular poem.

B: A black critic will pick up nuances in an appraisal of black poetry that whites wouldn't know just because they have not been on that side. The reserve is not true for blacks because, as I say, "we know the condition of your gums, having been so long between your teeth."

Q: I'm interested in the relationship between your poetry and problems in the world. Do you deal with global problems in your work? Do you feel a moral responsibility to deal with them in your work?

B: When I sit down to write, I don't say I feel a *moral* reponsibility here and I am going to write something that will save the world. But I have a poem called "The Near-Johannesburg Boy," for instance, that I wrote because I was listening to the news one evening and the anchor said that little black children in South Africa were meeting each other in the road and asking the equivalent of: "Have you been *detained* yet? How many times have you been *detained*?" I thought that was perfectly appalling. And I wanted to empathize with one of those children, so in the poem I impersonate a boy of about fourteen who begins, "My way is from woe to wonder."

Yes, I am interested in relations between the races, but it is always something personal and specific that will drive me to pen and paper. I am interested in the issue of abortion and I have a poem that so many people call the "abortion poem," which it is not. It is called "The Mother." I'm interested in the problem of young people committing suicide and I have a poem called "To the Young Who Want to Die Today." I like to say that poetry is life distilled. Anything that happens is grist for my mill.

Q: It seems to me you do bring your moral perspective and values to bear on the poetry you write. Your very vision informs how you approach a subject, for example, in "The Mother." To me that is a very moving poem about the pain a woman feels at losing her unborn child, and the pain that mother would always feel because of the loss of that child.

B: I am very careful to say when I read that poem in these times that it represents *one* woman's response. I make it plain that I know that not every woman would have the same response.

Q: Are you aware of the religious and human values that you put into your poetry?

B: I like that phrase "human values." Not everyone in this world of humanity is religious. Or some people might be, but they won't spell it out. I can't speak for the mass-murderers, of course, or the rapists and so forth, but I think that most people have some decency, some values. I like to ask groups of people, "Think about the groups of folks you have met. Weren't most of them decent?" Of course it just takes one to make things wretched for the rest of us, but generally people have values. That is my optimistic view.

Q: What do you think is the source of your values?

B: I had wonderful parents. My mother and father were cheerful. They subscribed to dignity, decency. They really loved their son and daughter and took as good care of us as they possibly could. My father was a janitor—not a Dr. Huxtable. I have never known a better person than he was, or my mother was. We had books in the house. My mother played the piano and composed pieces which I still have. We had dinner each evening at six o'clock unless my father was working two jobs—which sometimes he was, in those Depression times. We would sit around the table—can you imagine this—and talk about our day: what happened to us kids at school, to my father at work, and to my mother. My mother was interested in many things, so she had a lot of general conversation. I think that I was very fortunate.

Q: You were mostly a self-taught poet, weren't you? It wasn't as if you went to college and learned from poetry classes what works and what does not.

B: Right. When I was twenty-four, I went to a poetry writing class—we called it a class, but it was really a club. We talked about poetry, wrote poetry and read it to each other. We took our class very seriously. There were about seventeen or eighteen young people from the south side of Chicago. This class was begun by Inez Cunningham Stark, who was on the board of *Poetry* magazine.

Q: Do you think that a class is the best way to learn to write poetry?

B: I am glad that I had the experience of writing in a class, but I believe you can learn all you need to know about writing by reading.

Q: Do you think that that is how values will be passed on, from families and reading?

B: It would be nice if that tradition could be maintained. It is in many areas. Then there are the young people who rely solely on themselves or their friends. I really hate the idea of "peer pressure," but it's true that many teens are more interested in their friends than in their families.

Q: I was wondering if you write your poetry to be read aloud. Our class has been discussing how some contemporary poets don't write their poems for oral reading.

B: That's interesting. So many people say that they would rather hear my poems than read them themselves. I myself would rather read anybody's poetry than hear it read by even the best reader. That is because you can go back and forth in the lines, you know. And maybe at line eleven, you can say, "Hey, now I understand what the poet meant in line three or four." You can't do that or pick up the little gems of expression and savor them when someone else reads. Too much is happening in an auditorium, for instance. You are too conscious of what your neighbor is feeling.

Q: But your poetry seems more fun to read than poems by other poets who want you to look at a poem and not hear it. Your poetry has a nice sound. And it has voices in it.

B: Good! I am glad you feel that.

Q: I noticed so much alliteration, especially in "Goodnight Comes."
B: Yes. Too much, I know. That is my fault—over-alliterating.

Q: Is the alliteration intentional, or maybe a product of an oral tradition?
B: It is just because I love the sound of the words. I try to control my tendency to alliterate, but is it difficult. My daughter and I laugh about this because she has picked it up from me.

Q: I think that you and other black writers and women writers have particular contributions to make in our overall literature. Would you comment on what you think your contribution has been to the larger body of American poetry?
B: My contribution is that I tell the truth as I know it. To say what you really feel, what you think you know, is all that any writer can do. And it is enough.

Q: You have talked about reading being influential to you. Was the Bible part of your family reading? Has the Bible influenced you?
B: Yes, my family had a great respect for the Bible. Both my family and my husband's family respected it. You will probably all be shocked to know that I have not read all of the Bible. Has everyone here read every inch of it? [laughter]

Q: I have. Once I read the whole thing through.
B: Well, I should. I should. The Bible is part of education.

Q: Did you read much fiction or did you mainly concentrate on poetry?
B: I didn't read a lot of adult fiction. I used to go to the library and pick out the fiction for youngsters. I am sorry I did that because I would have had a better vocabulary, a better understanding of philosophy, sociology, if I had allowed myself more freedom in my reading.

Q: What other things did you read that interested you?
B: Emerson was one of my favorite writers. We had the *Harvard Classics,* and in those you would find Emerson and Benvenuto Cellini, and lots of English poetry: John Donne, Wordsworth, Swinburne. I used to swim in Swinburne.

Q: You mentioned Emerson. Has his writing influenced the things that you write?

B: He influenced my ways of looking at life. I remember that the essays "Compensation" and "Self Reliance" were my favorites. And I believed heartily in both. Whenever I was miserable about something—and you know that all children insist on being miserable a lot of the time—I would say, "It will all be made up for someday."

Q: When our class was reading "We Real Cool," we found out that the poem was banned in a Mississippi school early on because of the "jazz" reference.

B: I heard that some schools banned it in West Virginia; Mississippi, too?

Q: They thought the word *jazz* had sexual connotations.

B: So did a lot of people, but I didn't mean that at all. I meant that these young men would have wanted to challenge anything that was accepted by "proper" people, so I thought of something that is accepted by almost everybody, and that is summertime, the month of June. So these pool players, instead of paying the customary respect to the loveliness of June—the flowers, blue sky, honeyed weather—wanted instead to derange it, to scratch their hands in it as if it were a head of hair. This is what went through my head; that is what I meant. However, a space can be permitted for a sexual interpretation. Talking about different interpretations gives me a chance to say something I firmly believe—that poetry is for personal use. When you read a poem, you may not get out of it all that the poet put into it, but you are different from the poet. You're different from everybody else who is going to read the poem, so you should take from it what you need. Use it personally.

Q: You write a poem in private. It is your own feelings, your own thoughts, and then it becomes public property. And here you are now because of what you have written.

B: That is delightful. I like that idea. But when I am no longer here my poetry will still mean something to a person here, a person over there.

Q: Was there a time when your poetry was very personal—when you weren't ready to share it with the world?

B: No, I never felt that way. I remember thinking when I was thirteen, "Well, my poems may never by published, but at a certain point when I know that they are not going to be published, I'll bury them in the back yard. Then in a future dispensation, they'll be dug up and then perhaps they will save the world."

Q: In another interview you mentioned that you sent some of your poetry to Langston Hughes to read, and afterwards you said, "Even if he would have said I was rotten—which he didn't say—I would have kept on writing anyway." Where was that drive coming from?

B: I just love writing, putting my feelings down on paper.

Q: I understand that need. Someone can tell me I'm not writing well, and I keep on writing anyway.

B: But, of course, you won't be rotten because you'll want to write what is essentially yours, and you will work at it and work at it, and cross out all the clichés.

Q: How did you find what is essentially yours? Where does your vision come from?

B: Take my first book *A Street in Bronzeville*, which came out when I was twenty-eight. I just looked around me and wrote about the things that had happened to me on the block I was raised on. Those experiences on that street were essentially mine—at least my response to them was. You might remember a little poem called "The Vacant Lot."

Well, there used to be a three-story building there and on the first floor lived the people depicted in that poem, a woman married to an African prince.

Q: Who went away during the day.

B: I love that line about his "great white strong cold squares of teeth." I hoped that you would see each tooth—

Q: And a certain pride in those teeth.

B: Yes, because there are Africans just like that man.

Q: In that book and in your first book, I noticed that you sometimes see religion as a blinding force, as a force that keeps people from being self-reliant and changing their circumstances.

B: Really? I don't think I ever thought of it in just that way. What poem are your referring to?

Q: The "Soft Man."

B: Oh, that was about a young artist I knew, a painter who later became quite famous and hated that poem.

Q: In the poem he always has to be "cool," to talk to women in the right way, be seen in the right places. He shows this veneer all the time, and when he goes to church on Sunday, it is only to refurbish his veneer.

B: No, he was very religious. He found his salvation in religion. That was true in life, and I hope in the poem.

Q: So I misread it.
B: But he didn't want anybody to know. He kept that private.

Q: That he was a religious person?
B: Yes.

Q: And what about "The Preacher Ruminates Behind the Sermon"?
B: When I was a child, my family had a preacher—incidentally, the church was at the corner of the street where I was raised. My parents had deliberately bought a house on a street that had a church at the end of it, because they wanted us never to have an excuse not to go to church. If it rained, if it snowed, we could still get there.

Q: What was the name of the church?
B: Carter Temple CME, meaning Colored Methodist Episcopal. We had a preacher who said pretty much the same thing to his congregations Sunday after Sunday. A lot of us felt that he didn't really need to concentrate, and his mind could just wander wherever it wanted to. So I had him ruminating in the poem, thinking about God. One day a long time ago, I was coming into the bedroom where my TV was, to sit down and enjoy the "Donahue" show, and there was "The Preacher Ruminates Behind the Sermon" all over the screen. A little group of fundamentalists from West Virginia were talking about the poem. They felt that it was not a nice poem at all because you are not supposed to question God, not at all. You're not supposed to consider whether He is ever lonely or anything in that sense at all. But it is the preacher ruminating, not me. Of course, I am wondering.

Q: That is a lovely poem. I mean the notion that it must be hard and lonely for God to be set apart from and far above everyone.
B: Ministers have been very kind about that poem. They have said, "That's a nice little poem, but you just don't understand."

Q: When actually, on a very basic level, it is an attempt to understand God. It seems deeper than they are giving you credit for.
B: Trying to understand God—Are you supposed to do that, folks?"

Q: What do you think?
B: I believe in questioning everything myself. But I know that there are

many people who feel that concerning God you should just accept what you have been told—that's it—and go no further.

Q: Joseph Campbell says we have the notion of God to take into account everything we can't understand, everything we realize is beyond our ability to comprehend. What we don't know, we trust that God does know. I think that in trying to understand God, we are enlarging ourselves.

B: How about when some of the questions are answered—by science perhaps?

Q: Doesn't such knowledge bring us farther along the path to God by teaching us that much more about God? What do you think?

B: [Ms. Brooks waits for others to answer] I am interested in hearing individual responses. Each might vary just a little bit.

Q: I'll give you my personal response. I think that if you're going to love anyone, you need to have not a comprehension but an apprehension. You talk about apprehending a poem. Is *apprehension* a better term?

B: Maybe so.

Q: Is God just something I don't ever worry about and is just there? I can't love something that is just there. I question, and I have to because that's the only way that I can come to know God, to feel that I love God. Otherwise my relationship with God will be like my relationship with the law of gravity: I accept it, but I don't necessary love it.

B: I have never heard anything quite that interesting said on this subject. Your approach keeps you excited all the time, doesn't it?

Q: Poems that question God are interesting to me because that is my way of knowing.

B: Fascinating. Apart from this interview here, I would like to be educated. So may I ask you, have your settled within yourself the fact that little children who haven't had a chance to be evil come to such horrible ends here in this world? That is something that has always bothered me. Why little innocent children? Why should they have to suffer? Why should they be thrown up against brick walls or have their brains splattered by a gun butt? Have you settled that for yourselves?

Q: That is a question I have wondered about as I have worked with abused children. But I see the problem more as a result of people, not of God. People are cruel. These people are throwing children against a wall. Somewhere there is a lack of communication between God and these people. That is what the people have chosen to do.

B: But it has been said that God is all powerful. If that is true, why can't He or She—someone so powerful—put a stop to such evil? I am asking you because I am sure that you have given the question a great deal of thought.

Q: I personally have been taught and I feel that even though God is described as a just God, while we are here on earth there is going to be a certain allowance of injustice. But in due time when things come to a close, there will be justice and people will have to answer for their actions. And there will be a compensation made to the persecuted. I think people will be judged according to what they have been given, and those people who have been deprived will be taken care of. I have faith that there is more to the situation than just what I see. That attitude helps me to be more at peace.

I'd like to think that God wants us to wake up and see these injustices and do something about them. That's one thing I appreciate about your poetry. In many ways you are very honest. I think part of making things better is people like yourself who tell us, who make us see. We can legislate that there is not going to be discrimination, but until people love each other in their hearts, legislation won't make any difference.

B: It might be a long time before that happens, so in the meantime we do need those laws. I surmise that each one of you has done what I have done. You have told yourselves things that will make it possible for you to go on. What I have decided is that what I must do—what I have been doing most of my life, ever since I became conscious of need—is to be kind to people. Kindness is my essential religion, and I have governed my life by the light of that religion. I feel that no matter what the "truth" is, I can't go wrong with kindness.

Q: You have done much more than be kind. You've done incredible amounts to help people, to give them chances. I mean to encourage all those writers, all those kids, and to establish all those prizes. You are really an inspiration.

B: Because those kids are so talented. I have really enjoyed being here with you people, and having you talk and say what you are really feeling. That is so helpful to me. Thank you so much.

Gwendolyn Brooks: Humanism and Heroism

D. H. Mehlem / 1990

From *Heroism in the New Black Poetry: Introductions and Interviews*
by D. H. Mehlem (Lexington, KY: The University Press of Kentucky,
1990), 30–36. Reprinted by permission of the University Press of Kentucky.

DH: What leadership role do you foresee for Black poets in the 1990s?

GB: I believe Black poets will be *forced by events* into some form of leadership—although not necessarily will they wave their manuscript paper in the faces of the Black "community" screaming "We are now leading you, Black people!" and not *necessarily* will any one of them sit down to desk or table with the self-instruction "I shall now, via this manipulation of language, lead my Black people to salvation."

DH: Should the poets continue to direct themselves mainly or exclusively to the Black community?

GB: Many Black poets today do not "direct" themselves to the Black community, mainly *or* exclusively. I won't put a "should" on my answer. I'll just say that "essential" Black poets write out of their essence, which does not have to be spelled out at 8 o'clock each morning after coffee and orange juice.

DH: Should Black poets be personally as well as artistically involved?

GB: Yes—according to their strengths and their compulsion.

DH: Where should the emphasis be?

GB: On the poet's choice.

DH: Looking back on your life, would you change any of your major decisions if you could? Marriage, for example?

GB: Given old availabilities, I would have married as I married. I married the individual for sound reasons: dignity, volubility, belief in stable decencies (notably a home life and family life with "understood contours": certainly the Norman Rockwell view was "my" view, as I didn't know about African habits), sense of fun, interest in creating and raising children, sociability and an interest in "going out into life," a way-that-matched-mine of looking at Humanity and Eternity; and he, as did I, Wanted To Be A Writer. When you "get to be" my age (71) you have a large eye! You look over your diverse past, and you perceive that the diversities were all tending toward a resolving roundness: blotched, perhaps, nervous, maybe even tumorous—BUT THERE: round. This is not, nor should be, every woman's response. Each woman works with materials to hand or invented.

DH: What are the satisfactions of publishing your own work? What drawbacks, if any, have you found?

GB: Satisfactions of publishing my own work: "complete" control over design, print, paper, binding, timing, and, not least, the capitalization of the word Black. Do Blacks realize that they now have—since they got rid of the term "Negro"—NO capitalizations for their *essence*? Publishers refuse to capitalize Blacks. The Johnson Publishing Company of Chicago *does* capitalize Blacks, etc., but insists on capitalizing whites, etc., also. Whites *have* their capitalization: Caucasions. The Caucasians. A Caucasian. The Caucasian. "They spoke of Caucasian matters." Incidentally, the Johnson Publishing Company is Black.

We all happily, even though guiltily, capitalize Native American—which adulteration seems to me an insult to what we used to call "Indians!" I don't know *what* they should be called, but "Native American" suggests that until Amerigo Vespucci emerged, the "Indians" were as nothing. That is: they began to breathe and have being when whites came over to Bless them (and immediately to pollute them).

DH: "African American" has been proposed as a substitute name for Blacks. What is your opinion?

GB: The current motion to make the phrase "African American" an official identification is cold and excluding. What of our Family Members in Ghana?—in Tanzania?—in Kenya?—in Nigeria?—in South Africa?—in Brazil? Why are we pushing *them* out of our consideration?

The capitalized names *Black* and *Blacks* were appointed to compromise an open, wide-stretching, unifying, empowering umbrella.

Some Blacks announce: "That name *Black* does not describe *all* of us." Does the name "white" describe all of the people claiming its services? Those skins are yellow and rose and cocoa and cream and pink and gray and scarlet, and rust and purple and taupe and tan. Ecru. *But* that word "white," to those who wear it, is sacrosanct, is to be guarded, cherished.

Recently, one of our Black Spokesmen listened, with careful respect, to a passionate, sly, strategic white query: "Do you see a day coming when we can forget about EVERYTHING ELSE and just all be 'Americans'?" "Softly" answered our Black Spokesman: "We are *all* aiming toward that day, making progress toward that day—when we can *all* be Americans *merely*."

MEANING? Meaning we are to remember nothing. Meaning we are to renounce *or* forget our culture, our history, all the richness that is our heritage. Our new and final hero is to be Don John *Trump*.

I share *Family*hood with Blacks wherever they may be. I am a *Black*. And I capitalize my name.

DH: You did not mention disadvantages to self-publishing. Have you found any?

GB: Disadvantages? Let's call them "Irks." Disadvantages sounds final, indefatigable. The Irks *can* be defeated, granted a willingness to toil tirelessly—given reliable assistance—and given time. Irks: Distribution, Storage, Printers.

DH: Your powerful new volume, *Gottschalk and the Grande Tarantelle*, with its social and geographical breadth, presents some new developments in your work. You yourself recognize the poetry as "an advance, an approximation of what I'm aiming for." How would you describe this advance and this aim?

GB: Thank you for saying that *Gottschalk and the Grande Tarantelle*—which contains "Winnie," also available on its own volume—is notable for "social and geographical breadth." (You even said "powerful," D. H.) That pleases me because in this book I have combined what I *have* taught myself about writing with new decisions on what I want language to do for me, for my persuasions, for my compulsions, for my excitements. The title poem, "Gottschalk and the Grande Tarantelle," does exactly what I wanted it to do. There-are-The-Slaves: you are aware of the horror of their crisis *and* you are aware of the fact that human beings *will* break away from ache to dance, to sing, to create, no matter how briefly, how intermittently. Intermittently?—HOWEVER—like an under-earth river, that impulse to beauty and art runs fundamentally, relentlessly. Gottschalk, Elvis Presley, George Gershwin, Stephen Foster, etc., have molded Black exhilaration and richness into money-making forms. Inherent, also, is an ironic, begrudged semi-tribute to the abilities of such people to recognize greatness, to love greatness, when confronted by it. Also, I suspect that you have here a "perfect" snapshot of Louis Moreau Gottschalk, born in 1829 in New Orleans.

In "Winnie" I display Winnie Mandela talking, more or less, to America— talking to Outside. I say more or less because she is also talking to herself, she is also "talking" to her husband Nelson Mandela, she is talking to Her People in South Africa (and, to *some* extent, to Black people everywhere); she is also "talking" to Botha-and-such. I have tried to paint a picture of what the Woman must be like. The picture is "built" out of nuance and supposition and empathy. I figure she is composed of womanly beauty, of strengths female and male, of whimsy, willfulness, arrogance and humility, tenderness, rawness, power, fallibility, finesse, a "sweet" semi-coarseness which is the heavy fruit of daily oppression/fury/pain. *And* gloriousness!— glory. She is a glory.

Her Resolution in the last pages is what it should be. Interestingly enough, although certainly essentially hers, this Resolution is not alien to the impatience, now-shaplier roar, and beautiful self-respect of Today's Woman wherever she may live and under whatever stress she may be striving.

DH: The Black rage expressed in "Gottschalk" seems as vivid as that in "Riot," the poem first published in 1968. Do you see any changes in the Black situation in the United States, for better or worse, since that time?

GB: The "Black Situation" of this time resembles that of the early Fifties, with the Fifties' head-pats and spankings of what were then called "Negroes." With this difference: white power's nervous, irritable wariness. Because white power figures remember what a lot of Blacks don't: the late Sixties, which showed (mirabile dictu) that Blacks working together—or even, in *some* circumstances, just being together—are themselves powerful. Secret acknowledgment of that reality is one of the reasons that the phrase "the Sixties" has been shadowed of late, ridiculed, sometimes spat on: there is a jumpy desire for oblivion of that awareness of Black strength and potential resourcefulness.

There will be a betterment when (again) Blacks stop up-staging each other, shrinking away from each other, *selling* each other.

DH: The adoption of Black music by white musicians is an act that parallels somewhat the absorption of African art by modern European art, as in that of Pablo Picasso and his followers.

GB: Right!

DH: With regard to music, what would you suggest as a means of repaying the debt?

GB: I really can't tell musicians what to do. In "Gottschalk" I detailed what one of them *has* done, with the *scheduled* insinuation that other whites have done likewise. I am a reporter.

DH: "Winnie," 377 lines, as you tallied, is your longest work since "In Montgomery," 677 lines. About how much time did you spend writing it? Were there many revisions?

GB: "Winnie"—concept, thought, drafts, completion, polishing— overwhelmed a year. Revisions?—yes yes yes yes yes yes yes yes yes yes.

DH: Do you think that a poem like "Winnie" might influence the partisans of apartheid? Can a Botha be reached by poetry?

GB: The Bothas in the world cannot allow themselves to cry over poetry. They arm themselves against tears. Your official Nazi armed self against Jewish suffering. Such people subscribe officially to their arranged dogmas. There are, of course, exceptions to "all" rules. And sometimes it takes only one exception to weaken a prevailing poison, and to—sometimes— overwhelm it. Thus we poets (and here I include all clean pioneers, clean revolutionaries, clean Reporters) must continue our pinpointings, our nudgings, our "revelations."

DH: "Thinking of Elizabeth Steinberg"? Concerns the martyrdom of an abused child. It mentions the fact that Elizabeth is also your middle name. Were you making a point of your common humanity?

GB: No, I was not. That ought to be assumed, by the humane reader! I wanted to stress my conviction that the torture and murder of children must be stopped. That monsters must be invaded and "finalized."

DH: "Michael, Young Russia," the closing piece in Gottschalk, contrasts with the previous poem, "Thinking of Elizabeth Steinberg," by depicting a happy young man of twenty-one. You note that "Michael" was written in 1982 in Kiev, on a visit to that city and immediately after to Leningrad and Moscow. Does the poem's appearance in the new book, instead of in *The Near Johannesburg Boy and Other Poems* or in *Blacks*, reflect to some extent a response to Mikhail Gorbachev's policy of glasnost, the opening to the West?

GB: Michael seemed to me representative of a fresh, sincere, loving Russian-youth spirit. I wrote the poem in July of 1982, when I knew nothing of Gorbachev, glasnost, or perestroika. When I came back from my trip, I began to reach "Michael" to audiences. It was well received. I planned to bring it out in broadside form and then decided to include it in *Gottschalk*.

DH: For some time there had been talking—along the omniscient grape-vine—of adapting *Maud Martha* for the screen. Such a project is certainly overdue. Are there any literary genres you would like to try you have not as yet attempted?

GB: Yes. An epic. An honest-to-goodness epic.

A Conversation with Gwendolyn Brooks

Sheldon Hackney / 1994

From *Humanities* 15 (May/June 1994), 5–6, 36–38. Reprinted by permission of the National Endowment for the Humanities.

Sheldon Hackney: You are quoted as having said that being both an American and a black person, you felt you had the riches of two cultures as a writer, that that was a great advantage. This is really taking W. E. B. Du Bois's comment about the two-ness of American blacks, and turning it to advantage in some way. Do you feel that it has been an advantage to be black in America as a writer?

Gwendolyn Brooks: I'm wondering where I said that, but I believe I can still endorse it. It's not perhaps something that I would have elected if I had a choice.

Don't you think that you can understand my saying that it would have been right, perhaps, with a capital R, to have been born in Africa and stayed in Africa. I feel right about saying that to you. I'd like to quote from a couple of paragraphs that I have here that I've titled "On Being an American."

Hackney: Good.

Brooks: "In America you feel a little or a lot disoriented so far as 'being an American' goes. In the last few decades many Americans have learned an easy contempt for America; and true, a country that for so long endorsed slavery, endorsed lynching, endorsed official segregation, endorsed the Vietnam 'action,' and could be capable of judging political conspiracy acceptable, is not to be blue ribboned across the board. But traveling to other countries helps you italicize American positives. Once you get out of the country, whatever your woes, your wobblinesses, your confusion, your fury, you find that you are operationally an American. I myself am forced to realize that I am claimed by no other country. My kind is claimed by this country, albeit reluctantly. Furthermore, traveling teaches you that cruelty and supersedence are everywhere. Although it is not true that calling myself an American will instantly protect me from harm or detention anywhere in the world—when I was a little girl I thought this was true—still, that concept of

155

a large arm to lean on is implicit. Implicit: do not make plans to do any leaning. Remember for example, Beirut, remember Bosnia. It is not so easy for an American to abstain from 'being an American.' However roots-proud you as a Black may be, and my roots are in the sweet earth of Africa; when asked 'what are you' in Dublin, Devon, London, Israel, Iran, Ghana, in Moscow or Madrid, it is expedient and 'natural' to reply, twingelessly, 'American.' It is the only answer that will interest the questioner. The questioner is impatient. The questioner is ready for the Definer behind you. The questioner has small time, and no time for your efforts at self-clarification."

Hackney: I have had not the same experience, but I have had a similar experience of never having felt more American than when abroad.
Brooks: Yes, yes. It's interesting.

Hackney: I would guess from what you say that you would endorse the positive aspects of America, that is the ideal of America, but also caution Americans not to neglect their history. The history is there. It is what has happened. . . .
Brooks: Positive and negative.

Hackney: Positive and negative, yes. Is that an authentic stance for a writer to take?
Brooks: Well, I can't speak for other writers, I just said what I feel. Other writers are saying all kinds of things these days.

Hackney: You're exactly right. Let me go back into some of your biography. You won the Pulitzer Prize at the age of thirty-two in 1950 for *Annie Allen*. A very young age, a remarkable event; the first black poet to win the Pulitzer Prize. Did that change your life? Or your poetry?
Brooks: It made it possible for me to teach. I don't have a bachelor's degree. I have about seventy honorary degrees, but I always "blush" because I haven't Toiled in the Night for my honorary degrees. Having a Pulitzer made it possible for me to teach on college campuses. I've enjoyed being able to teach. I'm teaching now at Chicago State University.

Hackney: And there is a *Gwendolyn Brooks* Center there, is there not?
Brooks: Oh yes, and I hope you'll get to see it sometime. It's really nice. It's inspiring. It has an exciting future. But to get back to your question, naturally, when you get a Pulitzer—and I found out from a member of the family that you are supposed to pronounce it PULL-itzer (after all these

decades of saying PEW-litzer)—well, I was going to say, your name becomes, in my case, *Gwendolyn* PULL-itzer *Brooks*. (Laughter.) And there
are nice things about that. But in the late sixties the Black New Risers did
not consider such distinctions as glories to be proud of.

Hackney: It did not do you a lot of good then.

Brooks: Among young blacks, those rambunctious young blacks at that
time, there was often the feeling that there must be something wrong with
you, if you had acquired one of these gifts from the establishment. But that
was rather conquered. Because they decided—early on—to believe in me.

Hackney: You mentioned your lack of an earned bachelor's degree. What
was your education in literature like?

Brooks: I was given an associate literature degree from a junior college. I
know you're horrified to hear that.

Hackney: No, no, I think that's wonderful.

Brooks: In 1936 it was called Woodrow Wilson Junior College. Now it is
Kennedy-King.

Hackney: But you had parents who were both interested in literature, is
that right?

Brooks: Yes, we had lots of books in the house, and my mother said that
at the age of seven I brought her a page of rhymes, which she praised heartily.
Both my parents were supportive of my efforts as a writer, and of my brother's efforts as a painter.

Hackney: And that helped?

Brooks: Indeed it did. I was very fortunate.

Hackney: One of the things that all critics remark on in your poetry is its
remarkable command of all of the traditional literary forms, poetic forms. In
fact, you write quite complex verse forms and use incredible meters and
rhyme schemes. Where did that all come from? Did you work at that quite
consciously when you were young?

Brooks: We had the Harvard Classics, for instance, at our home. You'll be
interested in this, I think. My father had given the Harvard Classics to my
mother, complete with a bookcase which I have now in my bedroom, for a
wedding present. And there's lots of poetry in that set, as you know.

Hackney: Indeed.

Brooks: I read English poetry, American poetry, lots of essays. One of my favorites was Emerson. I got a lot of value out of essays like "Compensation" and "Self-Reliance."

Hackney: Those good nineteenth-century virtues that are all there. Would you recommend that sort of steeping in the literary tradition for a current course?

Brooks: I tell young writers today, of whom I see such a lot, that they should read everything. And I like to add to my adventures with the Harvard Classics, a little book called *Caroling Dusk*. I found that in a library, the Forrestville Public Library a block and a half away from my home. And there I learned about the work of Langston Hughes and Sterling Brown.

Hackney: And Dunbar.

Brooks: And the two Cotters, Joseph Cotter Senior and Junior. Countee Cullen. Claude McKay.

Hackney: Yes.

Brooks: And I was fascinated to find out that not only Paul Dunbar, whose work my father recited to my brother and myself, but all these other Black people were writing poetry and publishing it.

Hackney: Was that important to you when you were young?

Brooks: Absolutely. That was about the age of fifteen that I discovered these folks. In book form, I mean!

Hackney: Were you already literary?

Brooks: Well, as I said, my mother told me that I started writing at the age of seven. I do know that my first four poems to be printed were printed in the *Hyde Parker*. I sent them to the editor. He didn't know I was eleven, and just went ahead and published these four poems.

Hackney: That's wonderful.

Brooks: Very encouraging!

Hackney: One of the poems published in your book *Blacks*, "The Chicago Picasso," begins with a line that I would love you to explain—indeed, maybe this is the meaning of the whole poem, that is: "Does man love Art? Man visits Art, but squirms." Is that about the function of art in life, and what is the function of art?

Brooks: Well, you know the occasion was the unveiling of the Chicago Picasso here. Does man love art? Man visits art. (I wish we could find a word that meant man and woman. If you ever come up with one, let me know.) Does man love art? Well you see, Chicago people had been saying such horrible things about this piece of art, and somebody said that it had always been known that Picasso hated Chicago—

Hackney: That's right.

Brooks: —and that he had chosen this way of expressing his contempt. Other people were saying that they would have preferred a statue of Ernie Banks to this thing. So, in sort of mock exasperation, I'm saying, "Does man love Art? Man visits Art, but squirms. Art hurts. Art urges voyages—"I love that line because I think it is true.

Hackney: It is absolutely right.

Brooks: —and it is easier to stay at home, the nice beer ready. In common-rooms we belch, or sniff, or scratch. Are raw. "But we must cook ourselves and style ourselves. . . ."

Hackney: I like that line also.

Brooks: Et cetera, et cetera. Does that help?

Hackney: It does indeed, but now bring it back to the rest of your poetry. As you're writing, are you consciously trying to make people squirm on occasion?

Brooks: Oh no, I never sit down and say, "I am going to make people squirm." First of all, I'm excited about something before I begin to write. And then I just put down on the paper whatever comes—that's the beginning. But I believe in a lot of revision.

Hackney: Then you work and work on it.

Brooks: Yes, yes. Everything I've written, no matter how simple it may sound, has been agonized over; and I like to say that writing poetry is delicious agony—delicious agony.

Hackney: It is. But what about the voyage, the line about art sending people on voyages.

Brooks: Don't you consider it that yourself?

Hackney: Absolutely.

Brooks: The enjoyment of art! The practice of art! Both are voyages.

Hackney: Indeed, it opens up new vistas and makes people look at things in a slightly different way, if it's successful. Are you, as you write, consciously aware of that effect on the reader?

Brooks: You know, I don't do all of this very conscious speculating as I'm writing. I'm just anxious to get the verse arrangement down, and then to ask myself over and over, is this really what I want to say. I don't want to imitate anyone else; I have a lot of admirations, but I don't want to sound like any of them.

Hackney: Let me pose a choice between two different branches. One, in which you are writing as a poet speaking to an audience and quite aware of your obligation, your social obligation if you will, as a poet. On the other hand, the other branch, is that you are writing because of some inner vision, some compulsion to express your own ideas. It really comes from within, and has very little to do with what effects those words have on whoever happens to read it. Is that a fair sort of division, or do those things actually go together?

Brooks: Well, I don't give myself any obligations when I'm writing.

Hackney: That's interesting.

Brooks: In this little book, *Children Coming Home*, I have a poem called "Uncle Seagram," featuring a little five-year-old boy named Merle. And I didn't say when I came to write this poem, well everybody is talking about child abuse, therefore I shall write a poem about child abuse. What I wanted to do was to present a little boy, in this case a little boy from the inner city—which is a phrase I hate—but any child might be saying this.

Hackney: Yes.

Brooks: But that, too, is not something that I told myself. I'm going to read this very quickly. "My uncle likes me too much . . ."

When writing that I just tried to feel how a little boy of five might feel in such a situation. Although we come in different sizes, we are capable of feeling for each other, and as each other.

Hackney: That's right. When I read that I squirmed.

Brooks: Well, good! I read it in lots of high schools and colleges, and even elementary schools. And almost always, some child will say to me, "That's going on in my family," or "That has happened in my family." So of course I refer them to their teachers for possible assistance.

Hackney: That's right. But that just comes out of your success when you sit down to write, rather than the newspaper and some sense of what social issue you should be writing about.

Brooks: Or a too present feeling of social obligation. I like that phrase.

Hackney: You mentioned earlier the late 1960s and the rambunctious youth in the movement. It was a particular time in our history, and some people writing biographical sketches of you have pointed to the second Fisk writers conference in 1967 as a turning point for you. Is that a fair assessment?

Brooks: Have I ever had an interview in which that question was not asked?

It certainly was a very special time in my life, when I suppose you've read that I went to Fisk University and got my first taste of what was happening among the young Black people of that time. They were unwilling to be integrated, they were interested in loving themselves and having some kind of accented family feeling. It was a very exciting time. I know that it's the custom now to laugh at the late sixties, but there were good positives there, and I think most of us are better for those that were.

Hackney: I think you're right. It had a bright side and a dark side. And the bright side undoubtedly outweighed the dark side. But the dark side was there.

Brooks: Well, certainly I'm going to thank you for saying "dark" side. (Laughter).

Hackney: Okay.

Brooks: But you keep reading "the black side." Have you ever stopped to look in the dictionary for the definition of Black and Blackness?

Hackney: I have done that actually, yes.

Brooks: Terrible. Anyway, I got involved with young black people. I started a workshop—a writing workshop—for some youngsters that I met through Oscar Brown, Jr. Ever heard of him?

Hackney: Yes.

Brooks: He had created a very wonderful show out of the talents of these young Blacks who called themselves the Blackstone Rangers. This show was very well received here in Chicago until authorities decided it was not a good thing that it was so popular, and shut it down. But there were some dancers and singers who wrote also, and I started a workshop for them. That is how I got whatever reputation I still have as a red-hot revolutionary. I know that sounds ridiculous to you, but. . . .

Hackney: No, I think there is, in fact, a very strong sense of social commitment running all the way through your poetry, or sense of injustice that is there. The reason I ask the question is this notion that your poetry before 1967 is descriptive of the black experience but not alert to the injustice, whereas afterwards it is committed, more activist. . . .

Brooks: But you know, that is absolutely not true.

Hackney: Thank you.

Brooks: Many of the poems that I'm reading on stages now come from my very first book, and are considered "social." I dread saying political.

Hackney: But it is there.

Brooks: Yes, I think so. I've always had a—what do you want to call it?—social feeling, I've always felt for people.

Hackney: That is very much in your poetry, and I suppose that is one of the reasons that people think that one of the continuing themes in your poetry is humanity, or caring.

Brooks: Good, good.

Hackney: Which you would like, would you not?

Brooks: Yes, I do.

Hackney: The other thing one hears is that it is also heroic. I'm a historian so I'm not quite sure in what ways literary scholars use the word "heroic," but I think what is meant is not simply that you write about heroes but that you are after very large themes, on a grand scale, especially in your work most recently. Is that a fair statement?

Brooks: Well, most of the people who use that word when they're talking about me—forgive me for seeming to put this little halo around my head—are speaking of me as heroic.

Hackney: Yes.

Brooks: I'm not going to claim heroism.

Hackney: But there is this poem, "Winnie". . . .

Brooks: Yes, it's one I really like.

Hackney: That is heroic in its theme, is it not?

Brooks: Yes, yes. I don't know what you think of Winnie Mandela, but I have always considered her very strong and properly called heroic. She goes up and down in the public favor. Right now she's coming back up again. I claim "heroism" for her.

Hackney: Would your poem be different now if you wrote it knowing what you know now?

Brooks: I've never met her, but I feel that I came so close to nailing her down in that little book, that I feel I don't want to meet her. I want to believe that she is everything that I've put in that long poem.

Hackney: Yes, yes.

Brooks: You mentioned humanitarianism. I do have this little piece called "Humanitarianism." It begins: "Humanitarianism: of course we should love all the people in the world. Of course we should be humanitarian. What I have respected, in all my investigative life, is my vision of this world as a garden of varying flowers. Personally, I would not prefer a world of red roses only. Of white lilies only. Of yellow dandelions, only. Of purple violets, of black orchids, only. Of course I wish people had not been ripped from Africa, hauled over here in layers of chained slime, but even if I lived in a country of solid Black, I guarantee that it would give me pleasure to understand that in the world there existed other colors, other varieties, enjoying the fresh air I enjoy, and understanding that there was empathy, that there was the possibility of ultimate commerce."

Hackney: That's wonderful. So you relish the diversity that one finds in the world, and even in the United States.

Brooks: Yes.

Hackney: Are you optimistic about the future?

Brooks: Yes, I am an optimistic person. I am optimistic. There are so many excellences. And so much real love in the world. I have observed this over and over again, and even in these ticklish times, I am observing it. So I am optimistic, but my eyes are not blind to present horrors and I say frankly to you, that it seems to me that this is one of the worst of times for Black and White relations.

Hackney: In America?

Brooks: Well, anywhere. Listen to what Vladimir Zhirinovsky is saying.

Hackney: That's frightening.

Brooks: Yes, it is frightening. I don't think he's being taken seriously enough.

Hackney: Probably not. And there are people in the United States who echo him. Despite that, do you think we will be able to work through that to identifying some common ground for Americans?

Brooks: Yes, I think so. But I can't give you a date on it.

Hackney: That's true. Let me press you a little bit more on the variety of flowers that you enjoy in the human garden. If they are to thrive together in this garden, do they need not only to be different and therefore lively, but also to have something that they share, some commitment to each other? Or some common values?

Brooks: I think that they should, that all of us should get to know each other better.

Index